T0113792

Rising to Royalty

Rising to Royalty

MANIFESTING THE BRIDE
OF CHRIST JESUS

BISHOP AUDREY DRUMMONDS, PH.D.

authorHOUSE®

AuthorHouse™
1663 Liberty Drive
Bloomington, IN 47403
www.authorhouse.com
Phone: 833-262-8899

Published by AuthorHouse 09/29/2021

ISBN: 978-1-5049-5392-4 (sc)
ISBN: 978-1-5049-5391-7 (e)

Print information available on the last page.

Other books by Bishop Audrey Drummonds, PH.D.

Bringing Forth the Sons of God; Walking Spiritual Maturity

God's Redemption For All; Being One in Christ

The Book of Revelation (Vol 1); Christ in You, the Hope of Glory

The Book of Revelation (Vol. 2) Chapters 8-13

Living in the Inheritance of God

Rising to Royalty
Manifesting the Bride of Christ Jesus

(Author)
Bishop Audrey Drummonds, PH.D.

(Edited by)
Michael R. Drummonds

Contents

Acknowledgment

To my life-long partner, husband, and best friend, Ronnie. Thank you for walking unhesitatingly and obediently in faith with me as I have pursued this mountain for the Lord. Your encouragement and strength to pull me through my trials when I wanted to give up has been a great blessing as your sense of humor rings out, "Don't worry about the wagon, just load the mule!"

To each of my adult children, Greg, Ashley, and Michael. Thank you for believing in me, and giving me your wisdom when I otherwise would still be held in a bondage of past religious theologies that weren't truth, but simply tradition carried through time. Thank you also for your support in ministry, missions, editing, web design, and for your listening heart that allows me to share my voice that loves each of you very much.

To my dear friend Karen Kingsley. Thank you for coming along side me as a sister in Christ to help unveil the many facets of Father's heart in His people, land, nations, language, culture, and customs. We have traveled throughout the generations of time as we have spent lengthy hours in prayer, research, and pilgrimages around the world, speaking decrees of blessings into the earth and reclaiming the surrendered grounds the enemy has tried to control.

To my dear friend Janet Bassett. Thank you for being my life-long prayer partner. Being blessed in a lifetime with a friendship that speaks through time and space where ever we may be is a rare treasure and gift from Father I cherish.

Bishop Audrey Drummonds, PH.D.

To my dear parents, Frank and Lydia Thomas. Thank you for Life, Love, and the pathway of wisdom and direction to show me my Hebrew roots in Yeshua through your love in God and Jesus Christ.

All royalties of this book go directly back to planting seeds of faith and multiplying Father God's Kingdom work in the earth through Interior Coverings Ministry, a non-profit organization recognized as a 501(c)(3) by the federal government.

Interior Coverings Ministry website is: www.icministry.org. We can also be found on Facebook.

Introduction

Twenty years ago, I answered Father God's call for me, a woman, to go into ministry. I went through many trials: Loss of a career that I loved due to an incurable disease; Trying to function as a mother and wife while dealing with a disease that medical science had no answers for except to keep me on pain medication; Working through the shifting of identity, titles, positions, and the changes of time, and locations without forgetting who I was, all while being what other's needed me to be; The criticism of being a woman in ministry amidst a man's world of the Christian faith; And finally the thing that caused the greatest shift—hearing my doctor say, "You have CANCER!"

Through the tribulations I dedicated myself to searching in His WORD to find the answers to the question many of us have, "What are you saying Father to me at this moment that you could not say at any other time in my life?"

As my fingers have walked back and forth through the Scriptures from Genesis to Revelation using many translations, Bible-search websites, Strong's Concordance, Bible dictionaries, and wisdom of many of my colleagues' own writings and teachings, I found many hidden treasures of knowing Father God in ways that I was never taught in Bible College or Seminary.

My first major question came after reading the end of the Bible, in Revelation 22:16-17, "I, Jesus, have sent my angel to testify to you these things in the churches. I am the Root and the Offspring of David, the Bright and Morning Star." And the Spirit and the bride say, "Come!" And let him who hears say, "Come!" And let him who thirsts come. Whoever desires, let him take the water of life freely."

My eyes would be drawn to the word "bride." My past included the blessing experiences of helping several "bride's to be" with their wedding preparations, along with performing several weddings as a pastor. From a woman's position of putting a wedding together there is an intense planning that usually involves several months, sometimes years, trying to make the perfect choice of attire, attendances, food, flowers, location, reception, music… With finances and working through the family and friend relationships, things can become filled with tension and frustration instead of joy. Most brides-to-be see this is their only day to be the perfection of elegance and beauty, like a picture of royalty coming to be wed to her prince charming. She doesn't plan to do it again, and she doesn't go into the preparation with the idea that if it doesn't work out she will get a divorce. This is just not the heart of most women. We dream as little girls to be loved and to be seen as the princess in a man's heart, first to her father, and then to her beloved. This is how Father God created women…to be drawn to LOVE.

As a woman I realized that I had heard that Jesus was coming back for a bride, the church, yet I had never heard a male pastor teach on how a bride makes herself ready other than to accept Jesus as their Lord and Savior so they could go to Heaven. This is a good message for when we die, but did Jesus want us to prepare ourselves for our bodily death, or for His return? In 2 Peter 3:12, the Apostle Peter says, *"As **you** look forward to the day of God and (you) speed its coming."* Following through with that thought we find Scripture also says:

*"I delight greatly in the Lord; my soul rejoices in my God. For he has clothed me with garments of salvation and arrayed me in a robe of his righteousness, as a bridegroom adorns his head like a priest, and as **a bride adorns herself** with her jewels"* (Isaiah 61:10).

"Let us rejoice and be glad and give him glory! For the wedding of the Lamb has come, and his bride has made herself ready" (Revelation 19:7).

"I saw the Holy City, the new Jerusalem, coming down out of heaven from God, prepared as a bride beautifully dressed for her husband" (Revelation 21:2)

In order to search out what the writers in the New Testament were teaching the church as the bride of Christ, we must understand the Apostles' teaching method. It is a teaching method that has been lost in our Hellenistic approach of the Christian faith that presently makes up about ninety percent of all churches around the world. This Hellenistic/Greek approach has kept the body of Christ from walking and living in inheritance as new creations in Christ, not later, but while in the natural body on the earth.

The teachings and corrections of Jesus and Paul taught in the New Testament make up 85% of what is found in the Old Testament. Their method of teaching was a form familiar to Hebrew Rabbis which are titles both Jesus and Paul carried. When Hebrew children were young they were taught at level one, called "Peshat" which is simply straightforward or literal interpretation. This level is basic understand and application. This is the level that most believers in Christ Jesus live their whole life in relationship to Father God. It would be like an eighty year old person living life with the comprehension of a ten-year-old.

The second level of Hebrew teaching is called "Remez." Much of the teachings of Paul and Jesus were at this level. This requires a reference to go backward to move forward. Jesus shared a lot of His teaching by referring to the writings of Moses and Isaiah in the Old Testament that we read in the New Testament.

The third level is called "Drash or Midrash." At this level, teaching is done in a round table format or discussion table. The Rabbi is more of a facilitator to encourage discussion. If a question is simply answered by a student, it is a sign to the Rabbi that the student is at the beginning of this level of teaching, but when the student can answer the question with another question, it is a sign that they have moved to a new level of wisdom and understanding that a Rabbi would discern in order to encourage the student to go to the fourth level.

The fourth level is called "Sod." It is where Father God hides His hidden treasures.

"It is the glory of God to conceal a matter; to search out a matter is the glory of kings. As the heavens are high and the earth is deep, so the hearts of kings are unsearchable" (Proverbs 25:2-3).

In John 10:34 Jesus responds to the religious leaders on a remezing/midrash level of communicating to encourage the next level of sod. "Jesus answered them, is it not written in your law, I said, you are gods?" He is remezing back to Psalms 82:6, *"I have said, you are gods; and all of you are children of the Most High."*

As Jesus says this, He knew they would finish the words of Psalms 82:7 in their heart which says, *"But you shall die like men, and fall like one of the princes."*

You see, a prince has the royal blood identity, but not the discipline and training to rule and reign with Jesus Christ.

"On his robe and on his thigh He has this name written: KING OF KINGS AND LORD OF LORDS" (Revelation 19: 16).

The bride, the church, the body of Jesus Christ is expected to rule and reign on the earth, bringing the Kingdom of God into manifestation. The bride will have an identity and heart understanding as a king and lord, not a sinner saved by grace. Paul writes to the church in Ephesus and the Colossians that Jesus is the head of the body which is the church. John tells us in Revelation 19:16 that His name is on the garment of His body, and He has claimed the identity of oneness with the thigh. This is the helpmate of Jesus Christ, for the bride has made herself ready to take the name of her beloved, and knowing how to BE the manifestation of His presence, character, and nature.

My prayer is for these teachings to be a blessing of remez, and midrash with others in the body of Christ to elevate and equip the unity of oneness in Christ Jesus that brings us to the root foundation of our faith, *"Hear, O Israel: The LORD our God, the LORD is one"* (Deuteronomy 6:4).

Chapter 1

Preparing for Market Place Ministry

"Herein is our love made perfect, that we may have boldness in the day of judgment: because as he is, so are we in this world."

I John 4:17 (KJV)

*E*very action we produce is rooted in the thought that produced it. There is a reason why our Heavenly Father commands us to take every thought captive to obedience, because if the thought is not captured by obedience unto the Father's heart, then by obedience unto the Father's heart, then we bring our ego into the picture, causing us to be at the mercy of our own limitations. Our thoughts will either make us or break us, advance or hinder us in our growth in the Kingdom of God. Wrong thinking will make a way for negative behavior (James 1:2-5).

Trials are not designed to take from us, but to advance us to the Father through the joy we are meant to find in the midst of the trials (Psalm 23). It is the Father bringing us a fresh way of totally depending on Him. The experience circumcises our hearts, the throne room of God, where He abides in us. When we partner with God, we partner with joy. Count it ALL joy while in the midst of trials for it is the joy of the Lord that gives us strength bringing us from glory to glory in the Kingdom of God.

When we lack wisdom, we need only ask the Father who is anxiously waiting to give to us generously from His abundance. Jesus did only what He saw the Father do. He released the vision the Father gave to Him from His inner most being. He identified Himself as I AM (Psalm 82:6), allowing the Spirit of God to flow like rivers of living water through His heart, creating a form by speaking the creative word (John 1:14). The Father said that we perish for lack of vision.

Because of surrounding themselves with the Tree of Knowledge, many believers do not claim their inheritance in His Kingdom that waits to be brought into the earth. Both good and evil from this tree will produce death. One may come faster than the other, but the end result is the same. The visions and dreams the Father gives through the Holy Spirit are finished in the Heavens and brought through into our atmosphere when we allow ourselves to rest in HIM. This is more than just honoring a particular day. Jesus is our rest.

In the intimacy position of rest, Christ Jesus allows creative LIFE to flow from our inner thoughts. Paul discusses this in Romans 7. A bride takes her husband's name and identity. The third word we say after "I AM _____" determines if we are resting with Christ or ego.

Before the Father gives us the vision, He already prepares the journey for us to follow. Nothing is impossible when we begin in HIM. God is LIFE, LOVE, and LIGHT. There is no darkness, negativity, doubt, confusion, or ego. The old man is dead and we are now new creations in Christ Jesus (2 Corinthians 5:17). We have been given the blessing that *"As He is, so are we in this world today"* (1 John 4:17).

All of creation is waiting for the children of God to become sons and daughters of the Father to do the Father's business on this earth. The world's problems are not race, religion, gender, culture, traditions, economics, government, or educational issues. The problem is true believers in Christ Jesus are still stuck in an identity crisis of two worlds—the old Adam they kill then resuscitate, and Jesus Christ who is killed, resurrected at Passover, then becomes a baby again in December.

How many times does Jesus need to be crucified before we begin doing greater works than he did (Hebrews 6:1-6)?

> *Father, you send me out to do market place ministry. My thoughts are creative LIFE, the WORD made flesh and dwells among men, for you have made your abode, habitation residence in me. Where I am, there YOU are also today. Let YOUR glory shine through me changing the atmosphere for your Kingdom wherever we go so that others would be drawn to YOU by the LOVE they see in me.*

Selah

Chapter 2

Spiritual Gifts

"Their responsibility is to equip God's people to do his work and build up the church, the body of Christ."
Ephesians 4:12 (NLT)

*S*piritual gifts are the source of much controversy among believers. This is interesting and something of a sad commentary, since these gifts are meant to be graces from God for the edification of the church. Even today, like in the early church, the misunderstanding of spiritual gifts brings division—splitting up, rather than building up the church. This resource seeks to clarify the confusion regarding spiritual gifts, and to simply explore what the Bible says about them.

In 1 Corinthians 12, we learn that spiritual gifts are given to God's people by the Holy Spirit for "the common good." Verse 11 says the gifts are given according to God's sovereign will "as he determines." Ephesians 4:12 tells us these gifts are given to prepare God's people for service and for building up the body of Christ.

The term "spiritual gifts" comes from the Greek words *charismata* (gifts) and *pneumatika* (spirits). They are the plural forms of *charisma*, meaning "expression of grace," and *pneumatikon* meaning "expression of Spirit." While there are different kinds of gifts (1 Corinthians 12:4), generally speaking, spiritual gifts are God-given graces (special abilities, offices, or manifestations) meant for works of service, to benefit and build up the body of Christ as a whole.

Biblical References to Spiritual Gifts

The spiritual gifts can be found in the following passages of Scripture:

- Romans 12:6-8
- 1 Corinthians 12:4-11, 28-31
- Ephesians 4:7-13
- 1 Peter 4:10

Identifying Spiritual Gifts

Although there is a great deal of disagreement over spiritual gifts among denominations, most Bible scholars classify these gifts into three categories: ministry gifts, manifestation gifts, and motivational gifts.

Five-Fold Ministry Gifts

The ministry gifts serve to reveal the plan of God. They are characteristic of a full-time office or calling, rather than a gift that can function in and through any believer. After Jesus ascended to heaven, He divided the gifts into five categories and gave them specific names: apostles, prophets, evangelists, pastors, and teachers. All five ministries need to be fully active in the modern Church for the purpose of equipping the saints to be participants in the coming return of Christ. Paul told the Ephesians that they had been brought into the church and were built upon the foundation of the apostle and prophet, with Jesus being the cornerstone.

<u>Apostle</u> – Apostles are like fathers and mothers to the Body of Christ, raising the members up as sons and daughters in the faith. The title apostle comes from the Greek word *apostolos* which means "a messenger, one sent forth with orders." It refers to one who has been delegated authority by another, especially for representation in a foreign land.

Apostles were the first leaders of the Church; they were commissioned by Jesus to initiate and direct the preaching of the gospel. While the majority of Christians agree that the title of apostle is reserved for those among the first generation of Christians, many Christian denominations continue in one way or another to recognize a continuing apostolic ministry. Many churches, such as the Roman Catholic Church and the Eastern Orthodox Churches, believe in the doctrine of apostolic succession, which holds that properly ordained bishops are the successors to the apostles. Other Christian groups, such as classical Pentecostals, consider the role of a missionary to be fulfilling an apostolic ministry. There are some Christians, however, who advocate restoring the Fivefold ministry, including the formal recognition of the office of apostle. Others would say that the office no longer exists.

An apostle establishes and builds The Church of the Lord Jesus Christ, the bride, however, throughout generations and translations, an apostle has been given a subservient role as a church planter.

An apostle may function in many or all of the ministry gifts. He is the "thumb," the strongest of all of the fingers, able to touch every finger.

Prophet – Prophets bring supernatural revelation and insight, giving vision of the times and seasons of God so that saints know what to do.

In the New Testament, the office of prophet is second only to the office of apostle (1 Corinthians 12:28; Ephesians 4:11). The prophet's corresponding gift is prophecy. Prophecy is "reporting something that God spontaneously brings to your mind."

Many, particularly Pentecostals and charismatics, distinguish between the "office of prophet" and the "gift of prophecy," believing that a Christian can possess the gift of prophecy without holding the prophetic office. Prophet in the Greek means to "forth tell" in the sense of speaking for another.

A prophet functions as God's mouth piece, speaking forth God's Word. The prophet is the "index finger," or pointer finger. He points to the future and points out sin.

Evangelist – Evangelists impart zeal for souls to be saved and equip the saints with wisdom and anointing in winning the lost.

An evangelist is called to be a witness for Jesus Christ. He works for the local church to bring people into the body of Christ where they can be discipled. He may evangelize through music, drama, preaching, and other creative ways.

He is the "middle finger," the tallest one who stands out in the crowd. Evangelists draw a lot of attention, but they are called to serve the local body.

Pastor - This term derives from a Greek word for "shepherd." Pastors are gifted to lead, guide, and set an example for other Christians. They nurture the Body of Christ with counseling, clothing them with Christ-like armor and garments.

The grammatical structure of Ephesians 4:11 leads many to conclude that teacher and pastor should be considered one term (pastor-teacher). Even so, the two terms are not interchangeable—while all pastors are teachers, not all teachers are pastors.

The pastor is the shepherd of the people. A true shepherd lays down his life for the sheep. The pastor is the "ring finger." He is married to the church, called to stay, oversee, nurture and guide. However, the sheep are not meant to feed off of the pastor. The pastor has a responsibility to make sure the sheep have green fields to eat from, not the leadership.

Teacher - Someone who devotes his or her life to preaching and teaching the Christian faith. When teaching is provided for the Church by God, two gifts are actually given—to the Church are given a teacher and along with the teacher come a divine capacity to teach.

For some denominations, teacher and pastor is often a shared office, but not always. The teacher lays the foundation and is concerned with detail and accuracy. He delights in research to validate truth.

The teacher is the "pinky finger." Though seemingly small and insignificant, he is designed specifically for digging into tight, dark places, shining light, and picking apart the Word of truth.

Manifesting Gifts

The manifestation gifts serve to reveal the power of God. These gifts are supernatural or spiritual in nature. They can be further subdivided into three groups: utterance, power, and revelation.

<u>Utterance</u> - These gifts **say** something:

- **Prophecy** - This is the "forth telling" of the inspired Word of God, primarily to the church for the purpose of confirming the written Word and building up the entire body. The message is usually one of edification, exhortation or consolation, although it can declare God's will in a particular circumstance, and in rare cases, predict future events.
- **Speaking in Tongues** - This is a supernatural utterance in an unlearned language which is interpreted so that the entire body will be edified. Tongues may also be a sign to unbelievers.
- **Interpretation of Tongues** - This is a supernatural interpretation of a message in tongues, translated into the known language so that the hearers (the entire body) will be edified.

<u>Power</u> - These gifts **do** something:

- **Faith** - This is not the faith that is measured to every believer, nor is it "saving faith." This is special, supernatural faith given by the Spirit to receive miracles or to believe God for miracles.
- **Healing** - This is supernatural healing, beyond natural means, given by the Spirit.
- **Miracles** - This is the supernatural suspension of the natural laws, or an intervention by the Holy Spirit into the laws of nature.

<u>Revelation</u> - These gifts **reveal** something:

- **Word of Wisdom** - This is supernatural knowledge, applied in a godly or correct way. One commentary describes it as "insight into doctrinal truth."
- **Word of Knowledge** - This is supernatural knowledge of facts and information that can only be revealed by God for the purpose of applying doctrinal truth.

- **Discerning of Spirits** - This is the supernatural ability to distinguish between spirits such as good and evil, truthful or deceiving, prophetic versus satanic.

Spiritual Motivational Gifts

The motivational gifts serve to reveal the personality of God. These gifts are practical in nature. They describe the inner motivations of the Christian servant.

- **Prophecy** - Those with the motivational gift of prophecy are the "seers" or "eyes" of the body. They have insight, foresight, and act like watch dogs in the church. They warn of sin or reveal sin. They are usually very verbal and may come across as judgmental and impersonal. They are loyal to truth over friendship, serious, dedicated.
- **Ministering/Serving/Helps** - Those with the motivational gift of serving are the "hands" of the body. They are concerned with meeting needs. They are highly motivated doers. They may tend to over commit, but find joy in serving and meeting short-term goals.
- **Teaching** - Those with the motivational gift of teaching are the "mind" of the body. They realize their gift is foundational; they emphasize accuracy of words and love to study. They delight in research to validate truth.
- **Giving** - Those with the motivational gift of giving are the "arms" of the body. They truly enjoy reaching out in giving. They are excited by the prospect of blessing others; they desire to give quietly, in secret, but will also motivate others to give. They are alert to people's needs; they give cheerfully and always give the best that they can.
- **Exhortation/Encouragement** - Those with the motivational gift of encouragement are the "mouth" of the body. Like cheerleaders, they encourage other believers and are motivated by a desire to see people grow and mature in the Lord. They are practical and positive and they seek positive responses.

- **<u>Administration/Leadership/Ruler</u>** - Those with the motivational gift of leadership are the "head" of the body. They have the ability to see the overall picture and set long-term goals. They are good organizers and find efficient ways of getting work done. Although they may not seek leadership, they will assume it when no leader is available. They receive fulfillment when others come together to complete a task.
- **<u>Mercy</u>** - Those with the motivational gift of mercy are the "heart" of the body. They easily sense the joy or distress in other people and are sensitive to feelings and needs. They are attracted to and patient with people in need, motivated by a desire to see people healed of hurts. They are truly meek in nature and avoid firmness.

The New Testament contains several lists of spiritual gifts, most authored by St. Paul. While each list is unique, there is overlap.

Romans 12:6 1 Corinth. 12:8-10 1 Corinth. 12:28 Ephesians 4:11 1 Peter 4:11

Romans 12:6	1 Corinth. 12:8-10	1 Corinth. 12:28	Ephesians 4:11 / 1 Peter 4:11
• Prophecy	• Word of wisdom	• Apostle	• Apostle
• Serving	• Word of knowledge	• Prophet	• Prophet
• Teaching	• Faith	• Teacher	• Evangelist
• Exhortation	• Gifts of healings	• Miracles	• Pastor- teacher
• Giving	• Miracles	• Kinds of healings	• Whoever speaks
• Leadership	• Prophecy	• Helps	• Whoever renders service
• Mercy	• Distinguishing between spirits	• Administration	
	• Tongues	• Tongues	
	• Interpretation of tongues		

Chapter 3

Trees in God's Garden

---

*"The LORD God made all kinds of trees grow out
of the ground—trees that were pleasing to the eye and good for food.
In the middle of the garden were the tree of life and the tree of
Knowledge of good and evil."*

Genesis 2:9 (NIV)

*I*n the garden God planted all manner of trees that were good for food, and the man and woman were free to eat of all of the trees except one: The Tree of Knowledge of Good and Evil. Eating the piece of fruit in itself was not the sin, but rather, the tree represented a reality that to eat of this tree there would be death. At the beginning of man's existence, we read in Genesis 2:9 that Adam was in a relationship with three types of trees:

- Tree of Life - could be eaten
- Tree of Knowledge of Good and Evil - told not to eat or would die
- All the trees in the garden of other kinds - could be eaten

All of the trees that God grew which were pleasant to the sight and good for food were acceptable for man to eat. Notice *"pleasant to the sight"* was a factor man was to use to determine if the fruit of the tree would be good for food? In the midst of all of these trees was the Tree of Life which could be eaten from, as well as the Tree of Knowledge of Good and Evil which was forbidden.

"And the LORD God commanded the man, saying, Of every tree of the garden thou mayest freely (as much as you want you may participate, enjoying what you taste) *eat: But of the tree of the knowledge of good and evil, thou shalt not eat of it: for in the day that thou eats thereof thou shalt surely die* (or begin dying)*"* (Genesis 2:16-17).

On one hand we have a grove full of variety that man could freely eat from, utilizing sight to determine which fruit to eat. On the other hand we also have two optional trees that man had access to: one that carried the fruit of life and one that produced death.

All the trees in the garden were distinct from both the Tree of Life and the Tree of Knowledge of Good and Evil. The Tree of Life was NOT the same nature as all the other trees that God allowed man to partake of as food. Likewise, neither was the Tree of Knowledge. There was something about the Tree of Knowledge that was more than *"pleasant to the sight and good for food,"* that if the fruit were eaten there would be death.

Man was placed in the garden by God before these three kinds of trees, and man's whole life was depicted as a matter of feasting on one tree or another. How man would live and walk was dependent on his relationship with ALL of the trees in the garden. Let's read again:

"And the LORD God commanded the man, saying, of every tree of the garden thou mayest freely (as much as you want you may participate, enjoying what you taste) *eat: But of the tree of the knowledge of good and evil, thou shalt not eat of it: for in the day that thou eats thereof thou shalt surely die* (or begin dying)*"* (Genesis 2:16-17).

In the past, theologians have illustrated these Scriptures as a man and woman walking naked in the midst of a beautiful garden full of lush vegetation, streams of water, loving animals roaming around, and huge, healthy trees growing with a variety of tempting fruit to eat.

Somewhere in the middle of this garden there were two trees that were unique in appearance so that the man and woman would know which one was the Tree of Life and which one was the Tree of Knowledge of Good and Evil.

My personal vision pictured the Tree of Life as unique with a root system at the base of the tree not going into the ground, and its appearance subtly shimmering in light that came from within the trunk and branches. The Tree of Knowledge I would picture as having a root system likened to all the other trees, but it too had some kind of unique glow or aura around it that would draw attention and interest. Where the Tree of Life was receiving its radiance from the heavenly atmosphere of moisture in the air, the Tree of Knowledge was glowing because it was feeding off the earthly nutrients that were radioactive. Today we know that radioactive materials can have life or death substance in them, but at this time in the garden I would picture the couple not even understanding what "life or death" meant since they had not been exposed to it. Therefore, they were dependent up what they thought was *"pleasant to the sight and good for food."*

So what does the Bible tell us about trees? When we read Ezekiel 31 we find that when the word "trees" is used it is not referring to bulk trees in a forest or grove somewhere with fruit hanging on it. Trees in Scripture are **representative of people**; even in the garden of God called Eden (Ezekiel 31:18). Scripture is full of the mysteries of God, and this is one of them.

Let's read Ezekiel 31:14-17:

"To the end that none of all the trees by the waters exalt themselves for their height, neither shoot up their top among the thick boughs, neither their trees stand up in their height, all that drink water: for they are all delivered unto death, to the nether parts of the earth, in the midst of the children of men, with them that go down to the pit. Thus saith the Lord GOD; in the day when he went down to the grave I caused a mourning: I covered the deep for him, and I restrained the floods thereof, and the great waters were stayed: and I caused Lebanon to mourn for him, and all the trees of the field fainted for him. I made the nations to shake at the sound of his fall, when I cast him down to hell with them that descend into the pit: and all the trees of Eden, the choice and best of Lebanon, all that drink water, shall be comforted in the nether parts of the earth. They also went down into hell with him unto them that be slain with the sword; and they that were his arm, that dwelt under his shadow in the midst of the heathen."

In the beginning *"the earth was without form, and void"* (Genesis 1:2). What caused the earth to become void was the fall of man. Man lost his glory when he went down into the pit (Ezekiel 31:16). When we understand the symbolism of trees referring to people, then included in all the trees in God's garden were the Egyptians and the Assyrians. Here, when God is describing something using the mouth of the prophet Ezekiel, He uses a language that is symbolic telling Ezekiel, *"Son of man, speak unto Pharaoh king of Egypt, and to his multitude; whom art thou like in thy greatness? Behold, the Assyrian was a cedar in Lebanon with fair branches, and with a shadowing shroud, and of a high stature; and his top was among the thick boughs"* (Ezekiel 31:2-3).

It is all symbolism describing people. Included in the midst of all these people (trees) was the Tree of Life (Christ Life) and the Tree of Knowledge of Good and Evil (Ego). These two trees were in the world, but not of the world like all the other trees.

The Tree of Life was accessible for man to eat of its fruit anytime he wished. It was heaven's own divine life brought into man's world and made available to him. In the Tree of Life, man was given the divine source of all life to eat freely of. His relationship with God determined how often he ate from this tree. With the Tree of Life, God invited man to find Him as the source and center of divine Life. In this union with God, man would become an indwelling power of life in the environment in which he lived (the natural and divine together at once). Man would be a heavenly spirit shining in the image of God while living on the earth. This life would radiate from man as it did from Jesus on the Mount of Transfiguration. *"And as he prayed, the fashion of his countenance was altered, and his raiment was white and glistering"* (Luke 9:29).

God gave man the power of LIFE in this tree also known as Christ. Man had access to eat the fruit of this tree freely, which would allow him to function in the celestial realm while walking on this earth and radiating in all of God's glory. Heaven's doors would be opened, allowing man to move and talk in the power of the Almighty, raising him up from any possibility of sin, corruption, or even death into the uncorrupted power of God. This was demonstrated by Jesus Christ when He rose from the dead in a body of glorification.

Eating from the Tree of Life was more than just eating a piece of fruit. The tree represented a tangible, heavenly realm called Christ with the power of an endless life—a celestial life allowing man to have access to heavenly things while in a natural world. The power and wisdom of God

In Christ Jesus we have been brought back into the garden of God.

16

would be wide open to man, allowing him to walk in the presence and glory of God while on the earth. The heavens (mind of Christ) would be opened to man without a conflicting battlefield of man's own logic and understanding. Man would walk and talk in the power of the Almighty.

Scripture directs us to Melchisedec as a person with the power of an endless life, who had neither beginning of days nor end of life (Hebrews 7:16), who abides as a priest continually (Hebrews 7:3), he lives (Hebrews 7:8). One of the chief signs of the Order of Melchisedec is LIFE.

The Tree of Life represents a people of a particular order, or class of trees, that man was banished from when he partook of the Tree of Knowledge. God placed cherubim with a flaming sword to guard the entrance to Eden and access to the Tree of Life. In man's unclean state he could not partake of the Tree of Life or be a part of the Order of Melchisedec. This order (rank/class of trees) has been kept secret, un-touched, for thousands of years until another priest came into existence after the Order of Melchisedec, Jesus Christ, to clear the way for man to partake of this glorious life (Hebrews 5:10).

"He that hath an ear, let him hear what the Spirit saith unto the churches; To him that overcomes will I give to eat of the tree of life, which is in the midst of the paradise of God" (Revelations 2:7).

The man that stood in front of Abraham in Genesis 14, Melchisedec, cannot die. He is a priest continually…he liveth (Hebrews 7). He is a man of a righteous order that has been there from the beginning. If we were born from above, we came from priesthood, a lineage that has no beginning of days, or end of life. This has nothing to do with our earthly parents.

This priesthood has always been there in the garden, but access had been guarded. Jesus Christ came after the Order of Melchisedec to open the guarded entrance for us to enter into the garden of God and partake of the fruit from the Tree of Life.

Before man had to leave the Garden of Eden, God gave permission to eat of ALL the trees including the Egyptians and Assyrians. He gave man the option to eat of the Tree of Life, but if the Tree of Knowledge was eaten, man would know "evil" and its opposite "good" bringing "judgment and death" into existence. God is the creator of all things including evil. *"I form the light, and create darkness: I make peace, and create evil: I the LORD do all these things"* (Isaiah 45:7). Man was allowed to eat from what was "pleasant to the sight," as long as it was being viewed through the Tree of Life. By eating of the Tree of Knowledge, man's judgments of what would be considered "pleasant to the sight" would be determined by "good and evil" instead of the fruit of the Spirit which is *"love, joy, peace, longsuffering, gentleness, goodness, faith, meekness, temperance"* (Galatians 5:22-23). When we begin to separate "this is good" and "this is evil" we participate in a Knowledge that has no life in it; it is critical based upon the opinions of man instead of LIFE.

In the midst of all the trees (people), God placed the Tree of Life (Divinity, Christ Life) upon the earth. This tree is in the world, but not of the world (John 15:19). It was given to allow man the opportunity to rise above the other trees and see from the eyes of God versus whether something was "good or evil."

When man ate of the Tree of Knowledge, he fell into a certain mindset, judging the other trees (people) and separating himself from partaking of the Divine Life that was right in front of him. The Tree of Knowledge utilizes the remembrance of the past to justify the future. It renounces the fact that TODAY is the day of Lord (2 Corinthians 1:14), and we are all children of the Most High God (Psalms 82:6). When we separate "this is good" and "this is evil" we participate in a knowledge that has no life in it but the opinion of man.

In Genesis 3:11 when God said, *"Who told thee that thou wast naked? Hast thou eaten of the tree, whereof I commanded thee that thou shouldest not eat?"* Adam's response was not simply, "yes, I ate from that tree." Instead, he told God, *"The woman whom thou gavest to be with me, she gave me of the tree, and I did eat"* (Genesis 3:12). Now we know that God already knew the truth of what the man and woman did, but like any parent confronting their child's misbehavior, God played along by saying to the woman, *"What is this that thou hast done? And the woman said, the serpent beguiled me, and I did eat"* (Genesis 3:13).

Notice that the "finger pointing" stopped with the serpent? The word "serpent" is the Hebrew word "nachesh" which means a "hissing creature." First of all, never in the creation of man have we known animals to be able to intellectually create and communicate by "words." For us to think that there was a snake in a tree that could communicate with "words" is simply revealing the level of man's ignorance.

Just as the trees in the garden were symbolic of people, so was the voice that the woman heard coming from the Tree of Knowledge. I repeat, the word "serpent" is used to represent a "hissing creature" which the dictionary defines as the drawing of the "s" sound from "his" to declare disapproval and separation. The phrase "he said" (Genesis 3:1) came from the mind of man, lowered from Divine identity to the level of the animal kingdom. This phrase is the Hebrew word "amar" which means to say, speak, utter, tell, declare, name, to say in the heart, to think, the creative character of God's word spoken into existence.

When the woman said, "the serpent beguiled me," she was not communicating with a literal snake, but the creative power of thoughts and words that were in existence coming from The Tree of Knowledge of Good and Evil. Where did these thoughts originate? I believe the answer can be found in Scripture where we read, *"and he said unto the woman"* (Genesis 3:1); then in verse 6 it says, *"and gave also unto her husband with her; and he did eat."* The man that God created was with the woman the whole time. It was to the man that God told not to eat of the Tree of Knowledge of Good and Evil. *"And the LORD God commanded the man, saying, of every tree of the garden thou mayest freely eat: But of the tree of the knowledge of good and evil, thou shalt not eat of it: for in the day that thou eaters thereof thou shalt surely die"* (Genesis 2:16-17). It was man who was created after the image of God having the ability to create anything using the power of words. The woman was communicating with the voice of the deceiver that came from man disguised as a serpent. For this reason, man did not question or stop the woman from eating of the fruit from the Tree of Knowledge because he had already justified in his own heart the "goodness" that would come by eating of it. *"And the serpent (mind of man) said unto the woman, ye shall not surely die: For God doth know that in the day ye eat thereof, then your eyes shall be opened, and ye shall be as gods, knowing good and evil"* (Genesis 3:4-5).

Before sin entered into creation, mankind had the ability to partake in all the trees in the garden of God, however, as they ate of the many different fruits from the many different trees, they were not to look for evil. If they did, they would automatically look for good. This separation of what is good and what is evil was a knowledge that was not to be part of the garden of God. After mankind disobeyed God, to keep them from being in an eternal state of judgment and condemnation, God in His mercy placed cherubim all around the Tree of Life protecting the TRUTH to make sure mankind had to go through the purifying fire called the "flaming sword" of God's WORD.

Today we are able to participate in the Tree of Life because Jesus Christ, as both man and God, overcame death, hell, and the grave giving all of mankind the inheritance of resurrected life (2 Corinthians 5:15). In Christ Jesus we have been brought back into the garden of God. We now have the ability to eat of the Tree of Life 24/7, receiving His divine power and grace as we partake of the life of Christ Jesus after the Order of Melchisedec with the power of an endless life. According to God's word, this man Melchisedec is a people that cannot die, but that live continuously. The details of how or where these people are in this world are wisdom that only God can provide.

Mankind's choice is not whether to be a sinner or saint; whether to go to heaven or hell; or even to choose to be a Christian or non-Christian. Jesus Christ redeemed all mankind from the penalty of sin. He paid the price by being crucified on the Tree of Knowledge, removing ALL power and authority that this tree could produce. It was cursed by the spoken word of God to forever by removed. There is no more debt.

The heavens are open for humanity to receive the inheritance of an endless life today while in their natural body just as the time before mankind ate of the Tree of Knowledge.

This is the good news that was preached throughout the New Testament. This is the mystery of God that all of the disciples, including Paul, were martyred for. *"And the graves were opened; and many bodies* (not just spirits) *of the saints which slept arose, came out of the graves after his resurrection, and went into the holy city, and appeared unto many."*

(Matthew 27:52-53).

The only existence today of the influence the Tree of Knowledge once had is in the creative ability of our imagination. From God's view, there is no more curse, no more Tree of Knowledge. The weapon mankind is to use for warfare is *"casting down imaginations, and every high thing that exalted itself against the knowledge of God, and bringing into captivity every thought to the obedience of Christ"* (2 Corinthians 10:5); *"forgetting those things which are behind, and reaching forth unto those things which are before, I* (Paul) *press toward the mark for the prize of the high calling of God in Christ Jesus."* (Philippians 3:13-14).

The Heavens are open for humanity to receive their inheritance of an endless life today while in their natural body just as the time before mankind ate from the Tree of Knowledge.

Romans 6:1-12 Amplified:

"WHAT SHALL we say [to all this]? Are we to remain in sin in order that God's grace (favor and mercy) may multiply and overflow? Certainly not! How can we who died to sin live in it any longer? Are you ignorant of the fact that all of us who have been baptized into Christ Jesus were baptized into His death? We were buried therefore with Him by the baptism into death, so that just as Christ was raised from the dead by the glorious [power] of the Father, so we too might [habitually] live and behave in newness of life. For if we have become one with Him by sharing a death like His, we shall

also be [one with Him in sharing] His resurrection [by a new life lived for God]. We know that our old (unrenewed) self was nailed to the cross with Him in order that [our] body [which is the instrument] of sin might be made ineffective and inactive for evil, that we might no longer be the slaves of sin. For when a man dies, he is freed (loosed, delivered) from [the power of] sin [among men]. Now if we have died with Christ, we believe that we shall also live with Him, because we know that Christ (the Anointed One), being once raised from the dead, will never die again; death no longer has power over Him. For by the death He died, He died to sin [ending His relation to it] once for all; and the life that He lives, He is living to God [in unbroken fellowship with Him]. Even so consider yourselves also dead to sin and your relation to it broken, but alive to God [living in unbroken fellowship with Him] in Christ Jesus. Let not sin therefore rule as king in your mortal (short-lived, perishable) bodies, to make you yield to its cravings and be subject to its lusts and evil passions."

Philippians 3:6-11 Amplified:

"As to my zeal, I was a persecutor of the church, and by the Law's standard of righteousness (supposed justice, uprightness, and right standing with God) I was proven to be blameless and no fault was found with me. But whatever former things I had that might have been gains to me, I have come to consider as [one combined] loss for Christ's sake. Yes, furthermore, I count everything as loss compared to the possession of the priceless privilege (the overwhelming preciousness, the surpassing worth, and supreme advantage) of knowing Christ Jesus my Lord and of progressively becoming more deeply and intimately acquainted with Him [of perceiving and recognizing and understanding Him more fully and clearly]. For His sake I have lost everything and consider it all to be mere rubbish (refuse, dregs), in order that I may win (gain) Christ (the Anointed One), And that I may [actually] be found and known as in Him, not having any [self-achieved] righteousness that can be called my own, based on my obedience to the Law's demands (ritualistic uprightness and supposed right standing with God thus acquired), but possessing that [genuine righteousness] which comes through faith in Christ (the Anointed One), the [truly] right standing with God, which comes from God by [saving] faith. [For my determined purpose is] that I

may know Him [that I may progressively become more deeply and intimately acquainted with Him, perceiving and recognizing and understanding the wonders of His Person more strongly and more clearly], and that I may in that same way come to know the power out flowing from His resurrection [which it exerts over believers], and that I may so share His sufferings as to be continually transformed [in spirit into His likeness even] to His death, [in the hope] That if possible I may attain to the [spiritual and moral] resurrection [that lifts me] out from among the dead [even while in the body]."

The Order of Melchisedec testifies that there are a people alive today living an endless life. We must be careful not to get technical or analytical, but receive the wisdom of God according to His Divine understanding of what this means. It is a life that is more than the Levitical or the Aaronic priesthood. It is established, yet incomprehensible to our intellectual understanding. It is a priesthood continually abiding forever.

Jesus was able to say, *"Before Abraham was, I AM"* (John 8:58). We cannot remember being born because we were not born. We have always been a part of a priesthood, the Tree of Life. God gave us the Scriptures to reveal a secret about ourselves that has been tucked away and hidden in the Tree of Life. This Tree is the Divine person called Christ of which Jesus Christ is the head, and we are the body (Colossians 1:18). *"I am the vine, ye are the branches: He that abideth in me, and I in him, the same bringeth forth much fruit: for without me ye can do nothing"* (John 15:5).

Col. 2:8-10:

"Beware lest any man spoil you through philosophy and vain deceit, after the tradition of men, after the rudiments of the world, and not after Christ. For in him dwelleth all the fullness of the Godhead bodily. And ye are complete in him, which is the head of all principality and power:"

1 John 4:16-17:

"And we have known and believed the love that God hath to us. God is love (unconditional, agape love)*; and he that dwelleth in love dwelleth in God, and God in him. Herein is our love made perfect, that we may have boldness in the Day of Judgment: because as he is, so are we in this world."*

This priesthood has the power of an endless life. Scripture tells us in Romans 8:11 (Amplified Bible), *"And if the Spirit of Him Who raised up Jesus from the dead dwells in you, [then] He Who raised up Christ Jesus from the dead will also restore to life your mortal (short-lived, perishable) bodies through His Spirit Who dwells in you."* The problem we have is an "imaginative" veil that crosses over the mind of the people. We spend so much energy eating with the other "trees," which is not bad, but it does not remove the veil of man's reasoning that allows us to partake of the celestial life that is in the midst of us, allowing what may seem to be impossible to the hearts of man to be manifested as the will of God.

The natural mind of man cannot understand that God would put a celestial tree in the middle of His garden (within man's heart) called LIFE that has nothing to do with intellect, calculations, reason, opinions, or logic. Eating from the "tree" produces only one thing: THE MANIFESTED LIFE OF CHRIST. This tree is the open heaven, divine wisdom, secrets that have been hidden that manifest the impossible into the possible. This tree cannot be understood by reasoning from the Tree of Knowledge. Reason does not comprehend that the man from Genesis 14, Melchisedec, is still alive today. Jesus said, *"Verily, verily, I say unto you, If a man keep my saying, he shall never see death"* (John 8:51). Logic mixed with the environment of intellect cannot comprehend what Jesus was saying.

Unfortunately, many will try to take of the Tree of Life with the imagination of knowledge producing death.

In Christ Jesus, after the Order of Melchisedec, there is no sin. It's not that sin and corruption does not exist, but within this order that is above sin, there is no sin (Romans 8:1). We have received by the grace of God a ministry, a priesthood, making judgments according to what we do. However, most people disqualify themselves by condemnation of right or wrong instead of dying to self and living unto Christ (Galatians 2:20). It is not a matter of being enticed by sin, but by believing in sin that we give way, allowing sin to have power via enticing and temptation.

The more we participate eating of the Tree of Life, the more we will be overcomers. *"He, who is able to hear, let him listen to and give heed to what the Spirit says to the assemblies (churches). To him who overcomes (is victorious), I will grant to eat [of the fruit] of the tree of life, which is in the paradise of God"* (Revelation 2:7 Amplified Bible). This is not "someday when you get to heaven," but the blessings of God that we have access to eat from today. Week after week God is feeding believers from the Tree of Life, forcing the powers of death to loosen their grip. Today, newborn babies don't know anything about death or sin. They have to be taught. It is the responsibility of believers to open their hearts, disassemble the old way of thinking, and be re-taught by the Holy Spirit that God has brought us into a different kind of priesthood. At the resurrection of Jesus Christ from the dead, we became partakers of a different tree that was not available to the Levitical and Aaronic priesthood.

Reality is: Jesus Christ is the Vine; we are the branches in the garden of God. In Isaiah 41:18-20 we read:

"I will open rivers in high places, and fountains in the midst of the valleys: I will make the wilderness a pool of water, and the dry land springs of water. I will plant in the wilderness the cedar, the shittah tree, and the myrtle, and the oil tree; I will set in the desert the fir tree, and the pine, and the box tree together: That they may see, and know, and consider, and understand together, that the hand of the LORD hath done this, and the Holy One of Israel hath created it."

Trees are symbolic of humanity which is made out of wood. In Scripture wood always is symbolic of mankind. They represent kings, kingdoms, nations, leaders, the church, individuals, the Tree of Life (vine and branches), and the body of Christ.

The **Shittah Tree**, also known as "Acacias," is a hardwood that repels insects. It is a very beautiful wood used to build the Ark of the

Covenant. Symbolically, it is not susceptible to demons or darkness. A tree that signifies the glory of God, His presence.

The **Cedar Tree** is one that is firm, strong, tenacious, and rooted. It does not easily decay. The size of this tree speaks of great statue among the other trees for it grows 120 feet high and 40 feet around. Unmovable, faithful to God.

The **Myrtle Tree** is symbolic of sweetness and beauty.

The **Oil Tree** is symbolic of olives that are eatable. This tree is filled with medicinal character oozing with a healing richness and an anointing that flows to others. People can be blessed from the excess of anointing from this tree just by being in its presence.

The **Fir Tree** or **Cypress Tree** is the largest of the pines. This tree was used for making musical instruments for worship. It is symbolic of great statue and nobility, a people that worship God in Spirit and Truth.

The **Pine Tree** was known for its lasting endurance, its ability to withstand all kinds of weather. This tree was durable and dependable. A people that stay strong and full of joy as they overcome obstacles in life.

The **Box Tree** comes from the root meaning, characterized by standing upright, high and erected. It did not change in appearance as it grew. This tree was strong, honest, and prosperous, a wood that was good to build with. Not unstable, but what you saw is what you received. These people don't talk with a double mind. They are rightful and righteous.

We read in Isaiah 60:13 &15, *"The glory of Lebanon shall come unto thee, the fir tree, the pine tree, and the box together, to beautify the place of my sanctuary; and I will make the place of my feet glorious...Whereas thou has been forsaken and hated, so that no man went through thee, I will make thee an eternal excellency, a joy of many generations."*

When God reveals to us in Scripture the symbolic mystery of trees coming together, we understand that He is not talking about a literal forest of trees, but a corporate people that make up His body.

In Proverbs 3:13-18 we read that the Tree of Life is Wisdom:

"Happy is the man that finds wisdom, and the man that gets understanding. For the merchandise of it is better than the merchandise of silver, and the gain thereof than fine gold. She is more precious than rubies: and all the things thou canst desire are not to be compared unto her. Length of days is in her right hand; and in her left hand riches and honor. Her ways are ways of pleasantness, and all her paths are peace. She is a tree of life to them that lay hold upon her: and happy is every one that retained her."

Proverbs 11:30 in the Amplified says, *"The fruit of the [uncompromisingly] righteous is a tree of life, and he who is wise captures human lives [for God, as a fisher of men--he gathers and receives them for eternity]."*

The Tree of Life is an answer to what is desired or prayed (Proverbs 13:12). People that have prayed and withstood the natural obstacles by faith, eating from the fruit of righteousness, receive the blessing of the Divine Wisdom of God.

Proverbs 15:4 in the Amplified says, *"A gentle tongue [with its healing power] is a tree of life."* People that take what is wicked (negative, controversial, good and evil), and convert those words into wholesome life, love, and light.

Isaiah 55:8-13:

"For my thoughts are not your thoughts, neither are your ways my ways, saith the LORD. For as the heavens are higher than the earth, so are my ways higher than your ways, and my thoughts than your thoughts. For as the rain cometh down, and the snow from heaven, and returned not thither, but watered the earth, and maketh it bring forth and bud, that it may give seed to the sower, and bread to the eater: So shall my word be that goeth forth out of my mouth: it shall not return unto me void, but it shall accomplish that which I please, and it shall prosper in the thing whereto I sent it. For ye shall go out with joy, and be led forth with peace: the mountains and the hills shall break forth before you into singing, and all the trees of the field shall clap their hands. Instead of the thorn shall come up the fir tree, and instead

of the brier shall come up the myrtle tree: and it shall be to the LORD for a name, for an everlasting sign that shall not be cut off."

Psalm 104:16, *"The trees of the LORD are full of sap; the cedars of Lebanon, which he hath planted."*

Song of Solomon 2:3, *"As the apple tree among the trees of the wood, so is my beloved among the sons."*

Isaiah 61:3 Amplified, *"To grant [consolation and joy] to those who mourn in Zion--to give them an ornament (a garland or diadem) of beauty* (life) *instead of ashes* (death), *the oil of joy* (anointing) *instead of mourning* (sorrow), *the garment [expressive] of praise instead of a heavy, burdened, and failing spirit--*

that they may be called oaks **(trees)** *of righteousness [lofty, strong, and magnificent, distinguished for uprightness, justice, and right standing with God], the planting of the Lord, that He may be glorified."*

Ezekiel 17:24 Amplified, *"And all the trees of the field shall know (understand and realize) that I the Lord have brought low the high tree, have exalted the low tree, have dried up the green tree, and have made the dry tree flourish. I the Lord have spoken, and I will do it."* Trees (people) will come to have knowledge of the ways of God.

The Lord says in Hosea 14:4-9:

"I will heal their backsliding, I will love them freely: for mine anger is turned away from him. I will be as the dew unto Israel: he shall grow as the lily, and cast forth his roots as Lebanon. His branches shall spread, and his beauty shall be as the olive tree, and his smell as Lebanon. They that dwell under his shadow shall return; they shall revive as the corn, and grow as the vine: the scent thereof shall be as the wine of Lebanon.

Ephraim shall say, what have I to do any more with idols (trees that judges, separates, and brings division to the body of Christ)*? I have heard him, and observed him: I am like a green fir tree. From me is thy fruit found. Who is wise, and he shall understand these things? Prudent, and he shall* *know them? For the ways of the LORD are right, and the just shall walk in them: but the transgressors shall fall therein."*

Matthew 12:13, *"the tree is known by his fruit."*

Matthew 13:31-32, *"the kingdom of heaven is like to a grain of mustard seed, which a man took, and sowed in his field: Which indeed is the least of all seeds: but when it is grown, it is the greatest among herbs, and becomes a tree, so that the birds of the air come and lodge in the branches thereof."*

Acts 10:39, *"And we are witnesses of all things which he did both in the land of the Jews, and in Jerusalem; whom they slew and hanged on a tree."*

Jesus died for ALL the trees.

Galatians 3:13, *"Christ hath redeemed us from the curse of the law, being made a curse for us: for it is written, Cursed is every one that hangeth on a tree."*

Mark 8:24 (Amplified Bible), **"And he looked up and said, I see people, but** *[they look] like trees, walking."*

Revelation 22:1-5 (The Message):

"Then the Angel showed me Water-of-Life River, crystal bright. It flowed from the Throne of God and the Lamb, right down the middle of the street. The Tree of Life was planted on each side of the River, producing twelve kinds of fruit, a ripe fruit each month. The leaves of the Tree are for healing the nations. Never again will anything be cursed. The Throne of God and of the Lamb is at the center.

His servants will offer God service—worshiping, they'll look on his face, their foreheads mirroring God. Never again will there be any night. No one will need lamplight or sunlight. The shining of God, the Master, is all the light anyone needs. And they will rule with him age after age after age."

When God is talking trees in Scripture He is not referring to what we see in the forest, but humanity. Today, we are the Garden of God, and we are the branch of the Tree of Life in Christ Jesus. This truth must be what we partake of and what we eat daily so that the resurrection power of Christ within us will be manifested, filling the earth with the glory of God.

Colossians 1:24-28 (Amplified Bible):

"[Even] now I rejoice in the midst of my sufferings on your behalf. And in my own person I am making up whatever is still lacking and remains to be completed [on our part] of Christ's afflictions, for the sake of His body, which is the church. In it I became a minister in accordance with the divine stewardship which was entrusted to me for you [as its object and for your benefit], to make the Word of God fully known [among you]--The mystery of which was hidden for ages and generations [from angels and men], but is now revealed to His holy people (the saints),to whom God was pleased to make known how great for the Gentiles are the riches of the glory of this mystery, which is Christ within and among you, the Hope of [realizing the] glory.

Him we preach and proclaim, warning and admonishing everyone and instructing everyone in all wisdom (comprehensive insight into the ways and purposes of God), that we may present every person mature (full- grown, fully initiated, complete, and perfect) in Christ (the Anointed One)."

Every person is a part of a grove, a part of a tree. God's word has not changed from Genesis to Revelation. He declared that His thoughts and ways are higher than ours. His word will not return void but will accomplish what He sent (Isaiah 55:11). He gave permission to eat of ALL of the trees of the garden (Genesis 2:16). He places the Tree of Life in the midst of the garden (our heart) for mankind to eat of (Genesis 2:9). The only Tree that God commanded for mankind to NOT eat from was the Tree of Knowledge of Good and Evil. It was the only tree that could produce death.

The good news of the Gospel of Jesus Christ is that the flaming sword that once guarded the entrance into the garden of God, now paves the way to the Tree of Life, established once and for ALL. The price of sin was paid completely. In Christ Jesus we are able to eat of all the beauty humanity gives us. We don't have to be religious or isolated. All that God gave humanity He said was good and eatable. Everything in this natural world is affected and completely dependent in the balancing of how we see the trees (people) in God's garden.

When we stand upright in righteousness because we have eaten from the Tree of Life, the atmosphere around us begins to harmonize with LIFE. The earthquakes, mudslides, hurricanes, droughts, etc. are all manifestations of the changes God is making in His garden. He is bringing forth the righteousness in each of us, coming together as one corporate garden or body of Christ: the cedar trees, box trees,

> *The paradise of God is whenever our spirit, soul, and heart are in oneness with Christ Jesus. (Matthew 22:37)*

myrtle trees, olive trees, oak trees, pine trees, cypress trees, Shittah trees, etc. Each of these trees have a portion of His fruit, His blessing, His prosperity that when combined with the fruit of the Tree of Life (mind of Christ) becomes a manifestation of the glory of God filling the earth today.

We were born from a priesthood after the order of Melchisedec which declares an endless life. It is the order of Jesus Christ. In truth, wherever we are IS the paradise of God. The condition of our heart and mind is His garden. We are His trees in His garden. He is the vine; we are the branches. This is not about some bush or mysterious place called heaven. The Tree of Life is alive today within each of us. We will know the tree by its fruit, not by intellect or reason. The fruit of everlasting life in Christ Jesus is who we are.

"He that hath an ear, let him hear what the Spirit saith unto the churches; To him that overcomes will I give to eat of the tree of life, which is in the midst of the paradise of God" Revelations 2:7…

Verses 11-17, Amplified:

"He who is unrighteous (unjust, wicked), let him be unrighteous still; and he who is filthy (vile, impure), let him be filthy still; and he who is righteous (just, upright, in right standing with God), let him do right still; and he who is holy, let him be holy still. Behold, I am coming soon, and I shall bring My wages and rewards with Me, to repay and render to each one just what his own actions and his own work merit. I am the Alpha and the Omega, the First and the Last (the Before all and the End of all).Blessed (happy and to be envied) are those who cleanse their garments, that they may have the authority and right to [approach] the tree of life and to enter through the gates into the city. [But] without are the dogs and those who practice sorceries (magic arts) and impurity [the lewd, adulterers] and the murderers and idolaters and everyone who loves and deals in falsehood (untruth, error, deception, cheating). I, Jesus, have sent My messenger (angel) to you to witness and to give you assurance of these things for the churches (assemblies). I am the Root (the Source) and the Offspring of David, the radiant and brilliant Morning Star. The [Holy] Spirit and the bride (the church, the true Christians) say, Come! And let him who is listening say, Come! And let everyone come who is thirsty [who is painfully conscious of his need of those things by which the soul is refreshed, supported, and strengthened]; and whoever [earnestly] desires to do it, let him come, take, appropriate, and drink the water of Life without cost."

This truth must become what we partake of and what we eat, the endeavor of what we pursue: *We are the garden of God and we are the corporate body of the Tree of Life in Christ Jesus, connected to the order of an endless life.*

We do not have to eat of the Tree of Knowledge which results in sickness, decay, and death. God's word will not return void. All that God gave man in the beginning, we can partake of NOW in Christ Jesus after the order of Melchizedec, the order of an endless life.

God gave us freedom to eat of all the trees in His garden except the Tree of Knowledge of Good and Evil. The way has been cleared by Jesus to eat of the Tree of Life, continually reaping the inheritance of an endless life. Today we are the branches able to receive the nutrition that flows from the root (Jesus Christ) to bring forth leaves that will heal and restore the nations (Revelations 22:2).

Selah

Chapter

Resurrection Life Today

"And he is the head of the body, the church:
who is the beginning, the firstborn from the dead; that
in all things he might have preeminence."

Colossians 1:18 (KJV)

oday we live in a world that is suddenly changing. What occurs in one country on the earth can suddenly have an impact on another country on the other side of the world. An earthquake can occur in Japan, but it can be measured by instruments in central Florida. Nuclear reactors are destroyed in one area, but the fallout consequence is felt around the world through the economic system.

Though we see things in the natural realm, which seems to be a dominating kingdom, everything about our lives is ruled from an invisible domain called God's kingdom. The invisible place that He resides in is within each of our hearts. The condition of our heart determines the power of the words we release in the atmosphere, giving power to either the kingdom of Light or the kingdom of darkness. *"For as he thinks in his heart, so is he"* (Proverbs 23:7).

Around the world most people live their lives within the control and manipulation of being governed by systems and kingdoms of this world. These include: cultures, religions, genders, life- styles, age, education, economics, and family values. Their hearts may say one thing, but their minds are being overruled by the outward reflection of their feelings and senses governed by the kingdoms of the world around them.

When we look at a person, we can evaluate their outer covering—their gender, age, culture, life-style, and economics— by the way they live and the way they clothe themselves. As a person speaks, we may learn more about their education and religion. This information allows us to compartmentalize an individual in our world, and it will be helpful someday when their obituaries are to be written, but may or may not be of any real significance to connect with.

However, when we allow this information to draw us into asking the real question of where Jesus Christ is in this person's life, we are offered the opportunity to connect with the heart of God. Is there a testimony of the mystery of God: Christ in them, the hope of glory? Is there an unveiling in their life that says, "As He is, so am I in this world. When you see me, you see the Father?"

People tend to keep their inner thoughts private, the expression of what goes on in their heads keeps them living in the past or in the potential of what the future holds. It is only when we subject our thoughts to the present moment that we engage our heart in the matter that is taking place now. It is at this moment that the Kingdom of God is energized within us, challenging us to come up higher in our thoughts than what our senses are acknowledging and dictating in our lives.

"Then said he, unto what is the kingdom of God like? And whereunto shall I resemble it? It is like a grain of mustard seed, which a man took, and cast into his garden; and it grew, and waxed a great tree; and the fowls of the air lodged in the branches of it." (Luke 13:18-19).

The Kingdom of God has never changed. We may hear words that doctrines and traditions have considered vital that have carried us through seasons of change throughout history, but the Kingdom of God is the same yesterday, today, and tomorrow. We may find ourselves comfortable fellowshipping with certain groups of people that have similar knowledge of God's testimony, allowing us to lift and edify one another in that knowledge, but this is not the fullness of His Kingdom. We must be cautious not to judge the difference, but to unite the foundation rock of God's Kingdom: The resurrected LIFE of Jesus Christ who is the head of the body of Christ (Colossians 1:18).

The life of Daniel in the Old Testament shows us that the Kingdom of God is a counter-kingdom to the kingdoms of this world. It comes, interrupts, and invades the kingdoms of this world very slowly, undiscerning as a small mustard seed, but ultimately, everything in the heavens, where God resides, will be ruled by it.

We read in Daniel 2:21-23, *"God changes the times and the seasons: he removes kings, and sets up kings: he gives wisdom unto the wise, and knowledge to them that know understanding: He reveals the deep and secret things: he knows what is in the darkness, and the light dwells with him. I thank thee, and praise thee, O thou God of my fathers, who hast given me wisdom and might, and hast made known unto me now what we desired of thee: for thou hast now made known unto us the King's matter."*

Proverbs 25:2 says, *"It is the glory of God to conceal a thing: but the honor of kings is to search out a matter."* God gives wisdom unto the wise and His knowledge to those that know understanding. These come from Isaiah 11:1-3, *"There shall come forth a rod* (Jesus Christ) *out of the stem of Jesse, and a Branch* (body of Christ) *shall grow out of his roots: And the spirit of the LORD shall rest upon him, the spirit of wisdom and understanding, the spirit of counsel and might, the spirit of knowledge and of the fear of the LORD; And shall make him of quick understanding in the fear of the LORD: and he shall not judge after the sight of his eyes, neither reprove after the hearing of his ears."*

The patriarchs of the Old Testament unveiled to us that the Kingdom of God is a counter-kingdom to the kingdom of this world. It sets up and interrupts the systems, governments, and kingdoms of this world by a system that rules from the invisible, heavenly realm, yet is so powerful, it penetrates to the heart of man without any surgical incision made to the flesh. It moves with an invisible, subtle force like a mustard seed planted from God, but in His timing, everything in heaven, earth, and under the earth will be ruled by the Kingdom of God (Philippians 2:10).

This kingdom is a position of rulership that will be an atmosphere of righteousness, peace, and joy released by the Spirit of Christ within man (Romans 14:17). Those whom God has given wisdom and understanding will receive more as God changes the times and seasons for His kingdom to be manifested in the earth through man. God's kingdom has nothing to do with economics, gender, race, cultures, education, or governments that dictate our natural world. It is spiritual.

Every spiritual influence or presence is looking for one thing; it must manifest itself to express itself. The Kingdom of God, being the most influential and powerful, invades, violates, and conquers all other spiritual kingdoms. God looks to the overcomers, those that have gone through trials and tribulations in their lives that have the testimony of

God's goodness, mercy, and grace giving glory to Him of their position as an overcomer. *"For everyone to whom much is given, of him shall much be required"* (Luke 12:48).

We read in Genesis 1:28 AMP, *"God blessed them and said to them, be fruitful, multiply, and fill the earth, and subdue it [using all its vast resources in the service of God and man]; and have dominion over the fish of the sea, the birds of the air, and over every living creature that moves upon the earth."* The position of mankind before the fall was to fill the earth with "God kind" or the Spirit of God while subduing and taking dominion over all other creatures or other spiritual beings.

> **God uses the overcomers in life to bring the Kingdom of Heaven into the earth.**

Scripture refers to these other spiritual beings as familiar, demonic, or antichrist spirits. When we look to fight the "demons" around every corner, we often miss the real battle that is taking place. *"For we wrestle not against flesh and blood, but against principalities, against powers, against the rulers of the darkness of this world, against spiritual wickedness in high places"* (Ephesians 6:12).

When Jesus Christ is our Lord, we become a part of His diverse, membered body called Christ (Romans 12:5). His body only has the Holy Spirit. Any other spirit that rules in His body grieves the Spirit of God in us. *"Know you not that you are the temple of God, and that the Spirit of God dwells in you? If any man defiles the temple of God, him shall God destroy; for the temple of God is holy, which temple you are."* (1 Corinthians 3:16-17). God is a jealous God and will not share His Temple, His throne, His Kingdom with any other spirit. So what are the names of some of these "other spirits" that will try to take over the body of Christ Jesus?

The spirit of: Depression, anxiety, low-self-esteem, loneliness, insecurity, hopeless, unhappy, disgraced, humiliated, worried, bitter, impatient, outraged, furious, repulsed, vengeful, vindictive, envious, jealous, intimidated, manipulated, disrespected, etc. These are words that express as "feelings" of what we may be going through in particular circumstances. Often, the medical profession tries to get patients to express their feelings to help with the diagnosis of what their body is troubled with. Unfortunately, the quick fix is to give a medication which usually carries with it side effects. The big picture is that the Spirit of God is not leading and guiding, and the house of God is being shared by other spirits. Ask yourself, would you allow a thief or child molester to come into your home, take up residence, and fellowship with your family, especially if they were unwilling to respect and change according to your family values?

A logical thing to do in our everyday lives is to lock the door to your house and car to protect against easy access for thieves to steal from you, yet most of us have been allowing thieves in the house of God whenever we speak the words "I am" that are contrary to who God is. *"Nadab and Abihu, (sons of the high priest Aaron), died when they offered strange fire before the LORD"* (Numbers 26:61). They had allowed other familiar spirits within themselves to come into the holy place of God's house.

The Kingdom of God is a counter-kingdom, a counter-culture. It comes and interrupts the kingdoms that have been established. If the words that believers in Christ Jesus are releasing from their thoughts and mouth are things like, "I am anxious, I am depressed, I am insecure, I am lonely, I am ugly, I am scared, I am fearful, etc." there will be a battle of Armageddon going on between their ears; between their "I" and who God says "I AM" in them.

The Kingdom of God is so powerful among other kingdoms that it is always looking to invade, violate, and conquer. Again, it comes as a small mustard seed, but will grow as the largest tree. It will transform the atmosphere of fear and darkness into glory and light by the faithfulness of His presence. *"We know that all things work together for good to them that love God, to them who are the called according to his purpose"* (Romans 8:28).

God uses the overcomers in life to bring in the Kingdom of God. Some things to remember are:

- The Kingdom of God is appointed (Luke 22:29). It is a Divine calling (1 Thessalonians 2:12).
- It is entered into through tribulation or pressure (Acts 14:22). It requires a change in thinking (Matthew 3:2).
- It requires a new birth to see it (John 3:3). It is eternal in its power (2 Peter 1:11).
- It is all spiritual (Romans 14:17).
- It belongs to the Father and His Son (Ephesians 5:5). It belongs to the Father and Christ (Matthew 6:29).
- Seek it first, and He will add everything to you (Matthew 6:33). It becomes the largest Kingdom (Matthew 2:32).
- It consumes and is unstoppable (Daniel 2:44).
- What it opens, no man can shut, and what it shuts, no man can open (Revelation 3:7). It does not come by observation, and it eternally abides in you (Luke 17:21).

The Kingdom of God is a way in God that, once it has entered in, cannot be stopped. It works as a spontaneous reflex. When we listen to the stories of the patriarchs, apostles, and Jesus Christ, we see the conversion that comes in times and seasons that cannot be stopped. There is a certain place, dominion, plain, and atmosphere that, when the Kingdom of God abides in you, even though it may begin as a small mustard seed, it will cause transformation out of you that will affect everything and everyone around you.

The omnipresence of God goes with you wherever you go. He will never leave you nor forsake you. There is NOT a little bit of the kingdom on this side of life and then we get the rest after we leave the body. Our body is the residence of His Holy Spirit. This is where God is. He gives us the ability and wisdom to rule and reign on this earth with His Kingdom authority. Christ is in you!

"Verily, verily, I say unto you, He that believeth on me, the works that I do shall he do also; and greater works than these shall he do; because I go unto my Father" (John 14:12).

"Beloved, believe not every spirit, but try the spirits whether they are of God: because many false prophets are gone out into the world. Hereby know you the Spirit of God: Every spirit that confesses that Jesus Christ is come in the flesh is of God: And every spirit that confesses not that Jesus Christ is come in the flesh is not of God: and this is that spirit of antichrist, whereof ye have heard that it should come; and even now already is it in the world." (1 John 4:1-3).

There are many in the world today that refer to themselves as Christians, but they don't consider that Jesus Christ is THE WAY, THE TRUTH, and THE LIFE. The play on words here is that they will consider He is a "way-maker," an example to be followed on having a relationship with the Divine. There is "truth" in this belief, but there is not power as an overcomer in this world. This concept may get you into heaven after you die.

It was the belief and eye-witness experience of the resurrected Jesus Christ from death, hell, and the grave that gave the first church in the Book of Acts the ability to receive the power of the Holy Spirit and to do greater works than Jesus Christ; healing the sick, and raising the dead. This is the works of the body of Jesus Christ, the church and bride of Christ should be manifesting in the earth today. *"Therefore, leaving the discussion of the elementary principles of Christ, let us go on to perfection, not laying again the foundation of repentance from dead works and of faith toward God, of the doctrine of baptisms, of laying on of hands, of resurrection of the dead, and of eternal judgment. And this we will do if God permits"* (Hebrews 6:1-3).

Jesus Christ is THE WAY, THE TRUTH, and THE LIFE to know God in a personal intimacy as Father. All other religions, doctrines, and theologies will show you God, but only by knowing Jesus Christ personally as the only begotten SON of God is the Holy Spirit able to release in us the words to call God ABBA, FATHER. *"And because you are sons, God hath sent forth the Spirit of his Son into your hearts, crying, Abba, Father"* (Galatians 4:6).

It is this identity of I AM that is unveiled in us by the Holy Spirit which allows the releasing of His authority through us that decrees, *"As He is, so are we in this world today"* (1 John 4:17).

Selah

Chapter 5

Discerning the Lord's Body

Knowing Love and Truth in the midst of Deceit

"And ye shall know the truth, and the truth shall make you free."
John 8:32

*H*ave you ever asked yourself, why does God need to hear from heaven in order to – forgive His people and heal their land? Is not heaven the abode of God? How is prayer and hearing from heaven connected?

"If my people, which are called by my name, shall humble themselves, and pray, and seek my face, and turn from their wicked ways; then will I hear from heaven, and will forgive their sin, and will heal their land" (2 Chronicles 7:14).

Heaven is not just a cosmological location of stars and planet visibility, nor is it just a place we go to after death. Heaven is where God is completely lived. Heaven is where the invisible reigns over the visible. Heaven is the state of being that over-powers the natural state of being. Heaven is where the Light is, and the earth is the shadow of it.

Most Christian's formula is to obtain the presence of heaven through this earthly shadow— by what we naturally see. However, what we see is the temporal, not the eternal realm of heaven where God hears our prayers.

God made man a spiritual being. Before the temporal formation, God created man in His image. In Genesis Two, after God created (carved Himself out of Himself) man, not just one person but all mankind, He rested. After He rested, then He *formed* man. God spoke first and created by His Word spoken. He gave mankind this same ability that the words we speak have the ability to take on a form. The rest is the period between the measures of eternity into time, spoken word into form, thought becomes creation, perception becomes reality.

There have always been only two men—the first Adam and the last Adam (1 Cor.15:45). Even though there is a plurality to God's creation, the fundamental is only one true person, either the first or the last Adam. Therefore, God took care of the problem of sin with the first

Adam before there was ever a problem, for the lamb (the last Adam) was slain before the foundation of the world (Rev. 13:8).

As God brought substance into Adam's presence and told him to name it giving it an identity that still exist, Adam was able to do this for all the creation except himself. God had to first let him experience his own limitations to creation life. Then God put man to sleep – death- in order to raise him as a new creation to see that without the Holy Spirit – woman- he can never bring forth the fullness of his God identity he was created to be creating mankind in the image of the Father.

While the first Adam was created as a life-giving soul with the fullness of all the intellect and emotions of the soul's realm, he was functioning in the earthly shadow of the life-giving spirit until the arrival of the last Adam.

The soul of man is a conduit, connecting spirit and body in its search for heaven and earth to be one. The manifestation of heaven in the flesh is determined by how well man's soul is functioning as this conduit. If the passions and emotions of the soul are divine expressions then there is nothing wrong with this manifestation being released in the body. But if the passions and emotions are based on intellect or what we see in the natural realm, then the eternal power of God is blocked from full expression. Our own reasoning of the situation limits heaven from manifesting.

The soul of man desires to be Holy, but cannot obtain holiness by its own will. God gave the living soul this desire, but its fulfill is dependent on His connection to the life giving spirit. The Life of God gives breath to the soul of man's desire to be Holy. Jesus breathed Holiness upon the disciples after the resurrection of Life (John 20:22). Without the life- giving Spirit of God the Holy inheritance of man cannot be obtained in the flesh.

> *God must hear from Heaven, the place of His abode to bring healing to our land. His desire is to commune with "His Image" in the earth.*

"God said, Let us make man in our image, after our likeness: and let them have dominion over the fish of the sea, and over the fowl of the air, and over the cattle, and over all the earth, and over every creeping thing that creeps upon the earth."(Genesis 1:26).

What did God say? There are many in the world that can quote Scripture and share the deeper things about God, but they do not have the experience of being born again. This is not about where one goes *after* death, but living a life *today* with the breath of God ruling and reigning within the natural realm. Only then can there be dominion over the fish of the sea, the fowl of the air, the cattle, and all the earth. Being born from above is a process that includes experiencing trials and tribulations, so that the life-giving spirit of God can be manifested through us.

Our spirit was saved at Calvary. Our soul is being saved moment by moment, day by day. Our body will be saved and transformed into His image. God is not a keeper of time. The transformation of the body of Jesus shall be formed as "us" in Christ. *"In this [union and communion with Him] love is brought to completion and attains perfection with us, that we may have confidence for the Day of Judgment (in the midst of our trials and tribulations) [with assurance and boldness to face Him], because as He is, so are we in this world"* (1 John 4:17 AMP).

The responsibility of believers is telling the nations the Good News of the Gospel of Jesus Christ—the Kingdom of God is within you. These are the prayers that God is waiting to hear from His people. Not prayers of, "please God, fix this or that; "please God take away the evil." God is waiting to hear from heaven in YOU.

You are the conduit to manifest heaven on earth. You are the lightning rod to plug into the power of the Kingdom of God and to transform the universe around you. We have been short-circuiting our authority to have dominion over the earth because we don't have faith that what the WORD says has the power to overcome our situations in our natural body. We each struggle with the "I'll believe it when I see it syndrome."

For over 2,000 years, the body of Jesus Christ has run from the authority they have because they have taken the WORD into their soul-ish realm and applied their own thoughts instead of allowing the WORD in them (the DNA of God) to rule and reign. We were told by Jesus to declare the Good News; their sins are forgiven (John 20:23); there is nothing one can do to separate us from the love of God (Romans 8:38-39); believe in what God has done for them and they will never see death (body, soul, and spirit, John 8:51).

Jesus sent believers in Christ to be servants, to take dominion over the earth by washing the feet of the world in His love, so that all things are His that he may *"crush under his feet all the prisoners of the earth"*(Lamentations 3:34).

God longs to answer and bring forth the manifestation of prayers, but we must first become the answer to those prayers by crucifying the flesh, so that the body of Christ (us) can be the conduit for the power of God to be released. It is about Christ in you the hope of glory (Col. 1:27), manifested in the body of Christ—one cell at a time. It is about allowing the unity of His body to be formed in the earth as He is: LOVE released without condemnation, separation, or justification (Romans 8:1).

"Let us (Elohim) create man (you and me) in His image (as He is, so are we). Go; subdue the earth; over take it" (Genesis 1:26). Everything that is in the earth is under your rule if you have truly been born from above. Jesus taught the disciples to pray a prayer we call the Lord's Prayer, but really it was a prayer to awaken our spirit into knowing that God is our Father and we are lords of the LORD. The prayer that Jesus himself prayed was not, "Thy Kingdom come, thy will be done," for Jesus already knew this was accomplished. Jesus prayed the following prayer in John 17. Is this the prayer of your heart when you commune with the Father?

*I have given and delivered to them your word (message) and
the world has hated them, because they are not of the world [do
not belong to the world], just as I am not of the world.
I do not ask that You will take them out of the world, but
that You will keep and protect them from the evil one.
They are not of the world (worldly, belonging to the
world), [just] as I am not of the world.
Sanctify them [purify, consecrate, separate them for Yourself,
make them holy] by the Truth; Your Word is Truth.
Just as You sent Me into the world, I also have sent them into
the world. And so for their sake and on their behalf I sanctify
(dedicate, consecrate) Myself, that they also may be sanctified
(dedicated, consecrated, made holy) in the Truth.
Neither for these alone do I pray [it is not for their sake only that I
make this request], but also for all those who will ever come to believe
in (trust in, cling to, rely on) Me through their word and teaching,
That they all may be one, [just] as You, Father, are in Me and
I in You, that they also may be one in Us, so that the world
may believe and be convinced that You have sent Me.
I have given to them the glory and honor which You have
given Me, that they may be one [even] as We are one:
I in them and You in Me, in order that they may become one and
perfectly united, that the world may know and [definitely] recognize
that You sent Me and that You have loved them [even] as You have
loved Me. Father, I desire that they also whom You have entrusted
to Me [as Your gift to Me] may be with Me where I am, so that
they may see My glory, which You have given Me [Your love gift
to Me]; for You loved Me before the foundation of the world.
O just and righteous Father, although the world has not known You and has
failed to recognize You and has never acknowledged You, I have known You
[continually]; and these men understand and know that You have sent Me.
I have made Your Name known to them and revealed Your character
and Your very Self, and I will continue to make [You] known, that the
love which You have bestowed upon Me may be in them [felt in their
hearts] and that I [Myself] may be in them. (John 17:14-26 AMP).*

Next time you get ready to pray to God for a certain situation, stop and envision a wall outlet in a building that is used to "plug into" electricity. If we were to put anything other than the correct "plug" using the correct wall "adapter" into that power source, we risk igniting the building or being lethally shocked, ending our life in the flesh

Christians have the power of life and death in their tongues (Prov. 18:21). A believer in Christ Jesus is supposed to be dead to the world and alive in Him (Galalians 2:20). Much of the destruction and chaos in the earth is not because of evil dominating, but because Christians are using the WORD as children playing with matches instead of BEING one in the body of Christ Jesus and allowing His LOVE, LIGHT, and LIFE to flow into the earth through them.

"All of creation is groaning for the manifestation of the sons of God" (Romans 8:19).

Is God hearing your prayers from heaven so that He can heal your land, your health, your financial situation, and your family? Out of the greatness of God's love for us, many of the answers to our prayers are not manifested because we pray from our own logic and reasoning and not from heaven, bringing the judgment of God into our territory.

"For the time is come that judgment must begin at the house of God: and if it first begin at us, what shall the end be of them that obey not the gospel of God?" (1 Peter 4:17).

"And the Lord said unto him, Now do ye Pharisees make clean the outside of the cup and the platter; but your inward part is full of ravening and wickedness Ye fools, did not he that made that which is without make that which is within also? But rather give alms of such things as ye have; and, behold, all things are clean unto you" (Luke 11:39-41 NIV).

"Do not call anything impure that God has made clean" (Acts 10:15 NIV).

"You know the message God sent to the people of Israel, telling the good news of peace through Jesus Christ, who is Lord of all" (Acts 10:36 NIV).

"God did not give us a spirit of timidity, but a spirit of power, of love and of self-discipline. So do not be ashamed to testify about our Lord, or ashamed of me his prisoner. But join with me in suffering for the gospel, by the power of God who has saved us and called us to a holy life-not because of anything we have done but because of his own purpose and grace.

This grace was given us in Christ Jesus before the beginning of time, but it has now been revealed through the appearing of our Savior, Christ Jesus, who has destroyed death and has brought life and immortality to light through the gospel. And of this gospel I was appointed a herald and an apostle and a teacher. That is why I am suffering as I am. Yet I am not ashamed, because I know whom I have believed, and am convinced that he is able to guard what I have entrusted to him for that day. What you heard from me, keep as the pattern of sound teaching, with faith and love in Christ Jesus. Guard the good deposit that was entrusted to you-guard it with the help of the Holy Spirit who lives in us" (2 Timothy 1:7-14).

God must hear from heaven, the place of His abode to bring healing to our land.

God cannot commune with anything—person, creation, or spirit that is functioning in a position less than "God identity."

"Do not call anything impure what God has called clean." Acts 10:15 (NIV)

If we try to pray as a "sinner saved by grace," or through soulish emotions, out of our ignorance, we are incorrectly using the power of God. This will bring judgment and condemnation, short-circuiting what should be LIFE-current of God in the flesh, found through the blood of Jesus Christ.

"They know not, neither will they understand; they walk on in darkness: all the foundations of the earth are out of course. I have said, Ye are gods; and all of you are children of the most High. But ye shall die like men, and fall like one of the princes" (Psalm 82:5-7).

"But let a man examine himself, and so let him eat of that bread, and drink of that cup. For he that eateth and drinketh unworthily, eateth and drinketh

damnation to himself, not discerning the Lord's body. For this cause many are weak and sickly among you, and many sleep" (1 Corinthians 11:28-30).

Let us serve as conduits of heaven, so that God's identity may be manifested through his Sons on earth.

Selah

Chapter 6

Culture Change Begins
in the Heart

"Her ways are ways of pleasantness, and all her paths are peace."
Proverbs 3:17 (ESV)

United States of America, we are in a position of choosing leadership to make wise decisions that will affect our lives and the lives of future generations. Over 2,000 years ago the government of this world was placed upon the shoulders of Jesus Christ by our Heavenly Father (Isaiah 9:6) who loved us so much that He gave His life for us (John 3:16). Do the leaders of our community in politics, business, education, and religions have this heart in the position they are serving in? Would they still be interested in the causes they seem passionate about if their salaries, titles, power, and positions were removed? Do you think they would even want the position if they had to provide their own funding? What about the CEO's of corporations, or leaders in full-time ministry?

Jesus Christ died on the cross to set all men free receiving no money, no title, no power, or position while innocently hanging on a cross for a cause that He was willing to give His life for. Do we have any leaders ready to step up to the plate? How can we expect our local, state, and national leadership to bring our country into a victory battle over economics, racialism, religion, immigration, majority, minority, rich and poor when the decisions they make for others contradict their own life decisions?

Christians are notorious to quote 2 Chronicles 7:14, *"If my people, which are called by my name, shall humble themselves, and pray, and seek my face, and turn from their wicked ways; then will I hear from heaven, and will forgive their sin, and will heal their land."* However, in quoting this verse to justify a means, they tend to skip over the beginning that says, "My people called by my name." Do we really know who our Heavenly Father is that we can do the Father's business as Jesus did (John 17)?

True Godly leadership must come as the personified wisdom of God, never to be separated from the Father's heart. It must be experienced as a woman experiences giving birth to a baby, not just intellectual knowledge. Personified wisdom of God is ALWAYS a positive manifestation leading to reverence for the Lord (Job 28:28). Those that teach God's word from a position of terror and destruction will not know true wisdom (James 3:13-18). They will not be leading from a position of knowing the Father's heart as Jesus Christ set an example to be followed (Proverbs 14:6-7, John 17). It is the Lord who gives true wisdom, and out of His mouth, knowledge and understanding is released (Proverbs 2:6).

America, let us not forget the law (The Torah teachings and instructions) of our Heavenly Father, who knew each of us before we were conceived in our mother's womb (Jeremiah 1:5). Let us trust in our Heavenly Father with all of our heart, not relying on our intellect and understanding of the circumstances our lives are in. If we will acknowledge Him in ALL our situations, seeking first the Kingdom of God founded in righteousness, peace, and joy IN the Holy Spirit (Romans 14:7), and not our circumstances, then He will direct our paths into victory, overcoming every situation in peace (Proverbs 3:6). This is a path of a Father's correction in love, not wrath that will bring happiness, health, riches, honor, and life (Proverbs 3).

So America, let us not seek the wisdom of people simply because they have degrees, money, or prestige within the community. Our Heavenly Father says their wisdom is foolish bringing it to nothing (1 Corinthians 1:19-20). As sons of God, children of the Most High God (Psalm 82:6), we have a responsibility to question who we have in leadership, functioning in the Father's wisdom— blameless and harmless, without rebuke, in the midst of a crooked and perverse nation. Do they shine as lights in the world (Philippians 2:15)? Are they willing to make decisions for our community without any personal gain, but only with the wisdom of our Heavenly Father manifesting the heart of Jesus Christ? *"The wisdom of the Lord is pleasant and all her paths are peace"* (Proverbs 3:17).

The atmosphere over our land is a response to spiritual influence, whether it is good or bad. Once the atmosphere is affected over a period of time it affects the climate. If that climate is prolonged, then it becomes a pattern of thinking and possible stronghold. The climate becomes a culture, a behavior, or a way of living. Our Heavenly Father has called us to break the cultures, climates, and atmospheres that we have created over Tampa Bay by seeking first His Kingdom (Matthew

6:33), letting every breath sing praises to Him (Psalms 150:6) as we count it all joy in the midst of our trials and tribulations (James 1:2).

This may seem too simple and silly, but it is the pattern Paul used to break the chains while in jail (Acts. 16), and it is today the pattern used in other countries that are predominately of other religions. While I was visiting Istanbul, Turkey, we would hear prayers sung over the city several times a day. It only takes one person to change the atmosphere, which will change the climate and the culture. God will use the trials and conditions of our life to reveal and introduce Himself for the purpose of our life and the circumstance of it.

Today, we have many in leadership that declare that they are Christians and can quote the Scriptures to justify their means, but their heart still has a piece of "what's in it for them." True, Godly leadership must come from the Father's heart to bring true change. It is the truth that our leaders know and have personally experienced as God's Divine intervention that will set us free (John 8:32). We will only hear true and right words from their mouth; not one syllable will be twisted or skewed. All the words of their mouth will be righteous (upright and in right standing with God); there will not be anything contrary to truth or crooked in them (Proverbs 8:6-7) causing a double-mind (James 1:8).

Will the true leaders that seek the Father's heart in leadership please step forward! Where are our leaders in politics, businesses, religions, education, and community organizations that are seeking God as King Solomon who prayed, *"Now, O Lord my God, You have made Your servant king instead of David my father, and I am but a lad [in wisdom and experience]; I know not how to go out (begin) or come in (finish)"* (1 King 3:7)?

Today, we have *someone more and greater than Solomon* (Matthew 12:42). Christ within and among you (Colossians 1:27) is the hope and glory for our community, state, and nation to set the captive free. Whom the Son of God sets free is true freedom, liberty, and justice for all (John 8:36).

"How beautiful upon the mountains are the feet of him who brings good tidings, who publishes peace, who brings good tidings of good, who publishes salvation, who says to Zion, Your God reigns" (Isaiah 57:2).

Selah

Chapter 7

An Overcoming Spirit:

Manifesting the reality of being an overcomer

---

*"Do not conform to the pattern of this world,
but be transformed by the renewing of your mind.
Then you will be able to test and approve what
God's will is—his good, pleasing and perfect will."*

Romans 12:2

There is an aroma of God's knowledge and His presence, manifested by us as the climate or atmosphere around us.

"But thanks be to God, Who in Christ always leads us in triumph [as trophies of Christ's victory] and through us spreads and makes evident the fragrance of the knowledge of God everywhere, For we are the sweet fragrance of Christ [which exhales] unto God, [discernible alike] among those who are being saved and among those who are perishing: To the latter it is an aroma [wafted] from death to death [a fatal odor, the smell of doom]; to the former it is an aroma from life to life [a vital fragrance, living and fresh]. And who is qualified (fit and sufficient) for these things? [Who is able for such a ministry? We?] For we are not, like so many, [like hucksters making a trade of] peddling God's Word [shortchanging and adulterating the divine message]; but like [men] of sincerity and the purest motive, as [commissioned and sent] by God, we speak [His message] in Christ (the Messiah), in the [very] sight and presence of God." (2 Cor. 2: 14-17 AMP)

These verses are not talking about people that are in a survival mode, waiting and pleading for Jesus to rapture them out or to take away their trials. This is not an attitude of deliverance from the circumstance, but an attitude of triumphal victory. Paul is using words that would have been familiar to the Romans: of having a triumphal march that would be seen after the victory of a battle, throwing roses in the streets as the soldiers and generals would parade in their chariots down the streets. Paul is trying to tell us that Jesus Christ has already won the battle of our circumstance and that we are the paraded aroma of that victory. He has already overcome, making an open display of demonic powers.

"For now we are looking in a mirror that gives only a dim (blurred) reflection [of reality as in a riddle or enigma], but then [when perfection comes] we shall see in reality and face to face! Now I know in part (imperfectly), but then I shall know and understand fully and clearly, even in the same manner as I have been fully and clearly known and understood [by God]. And so faith, hope, love abide [faith--conviction and belief respecting man's relation to God and divine things; hope--joyful and confident expectation of eternal salvation; love-- true affection for God and

man, growing out of God's love for and in us], these three; but the greatest of these is love" (1 Corinthians 13: 12-13).

Everything in our atmosphere can be shaken except faith, hope, and love. These cannot be taken away by external circumstances. No matter what areas of our life come and go—money, people, health, circumstance changes, etc.—what keeps us is the internal presence of faith, hope, and love. When we join in the victory posture (join in the party celebration) of Christ in us, the position where all circumstances have been overcome by the blood of the lamb, and we live today as new creations in Him. Celebrating the victory of an overcomer, we change the atmosphere of the world by the attitude of our hearts. We cannot help but have a joyful expectation of miracles.

This is the position that Paul is sharing in his letter to Corinth: while in the circumstance of worldly darkness and unknown, celebrate within you the victory that is found in Jesus Christ established by faith, hope, and His love.

Hope: an expectation with pleasure, or a joyful expectation with confidence. The inner being of oneself, Christ in you, is in a posture of joyful expectation and confidence.

Faith: the assurance (the confirmation, the title deed) of the things [we] hope for, being the proof of things [we] do not see and the conviction of their reality [faith perceiving as real fact what is not revealed to the senses].

Love: GOD, unselfish, unconditional, eternal.

Today, there is an atmosphere of the Lord coming and "bailing us out." This is not an atmosphere of joyful expectation with confidence, but an attitude of survival. We can change the atmosphere around us by lining up our expectations with the triumphal victory of what Christ in us has established already. We have within us the hope to display a great victory parade to the world.

> **Whatever climate or atmosphere we produce we also must live under.**

Without faith, hope, and love, we would all die quickly in our 30's and 40's from the conditions of this world. Besides the battles of territory that men fight, women would have no hope to survive the travails of bringing forth children. *"Keep and guard your heart with all vigilance (diligence) and above all that you guard, for out of it flows the springs (issues) of life"* (Proverbs 4:23). *"Whatever comes out of the mouth comes from the heart"* (Matthew 15:18). *"Death and life are in the power of the tongue, and they who indulge in it shall eat the fruit of it [for death or life]"* (Proverbs 18:21).

Faith, hope, love, and peace are spiritual substances. You cannot see them, grab them, or put them in your pocket, but these things are sustainable substances that keep your life. They are the Spirit of God that carries the visions He gives us while we are on a mountain top to be manifested in the valley. Without them, life becomes a monotonous, quick-ending routine.

What causes life to be a life worth living is what comes out of the realm of your heart—the place of your spirit. These things: faith, hope, love, and peace, only God can give. Without these things, there is no life apart from the existence of the animal kingdom.

Today, we have the ability to rise above the realities of the world into the dominion of LIFE. If our life is about paying our bills and maintaining our existence until we die, then the triumphal environment, fragrance and essence of God's life in us is no longer part of our climate. Therefore, whatever climate or atmosphere we produce, we also live under. If we live in an atmosphere of fear, victimization, and survival then we will attract the product of what we produce.

What are the simple truths we can live in today so that our inheritance, what we have already been given through Christ Jesus, can be displayed and manifested and change our atmosphere to the victory parade fragrance of His presence?

What is the difference between survival and victory? Do we want to go through our trials again? When we stay in survival mode, we will go through the trials again and again. When we have victory, we have conquered and overcome.

Everything has a spirit form, an essence form.

Love, hate, joy, anger, prosperity, poverty are spirit forms of principalities and powers. Everything forms out of the domain of spirit.

"For we wrestle not against flesh and blood, but against principalities, against powers, against the rulers of the darkness of this world, against spiritual wickedness in high places" (Ephesians 6:12).

Everything forms out of the domain of the spirit.

"For in Him the whole fullness of Deity (the Godhead) continues to dwell in bodily form [giving complete expression of the divine nature. And you are in Him, made full and having come to fullness of life [in Christ you too are filled with the Godhead--Father, Son and Holy Spirit—and reach full spiritual stature]. And He is the Head of all rules and authority [of every angelic principality and power]. In Him also you were circumcised with a circumcision not made with hands, but in a [spiritual] circumcision [performed by] Christ by stripping off the body of the flesh (the whole corrupt, carnal nature with its passions and lusts). [Thus you were circumcised when] you were buried with Him in [your] baptism, in which you were also raised with Him [to a new life] through [your] faith in the working of God [as displayed] when He flesh (your sensuality, your sinful carnal nature), [God] brought to life together with [Christ], having [freely] forgiven us all our transgressions, having cancelled and blotted out and wiped away the handwriting of the note (bond) with its legal decrees and demands which was in force and stood against us (hostile to us). This [note with its regulations, decrees, and demands] He set aside and cleared raised Him up from the dead. And you who were dead in trespasses and in the uncircumcision of your completely out of our way by nailing it to [His] cross. [God] disarmed the principalities and powers that were ranged against us and made a bold display and public example of them, in triumphing over them in Him and in it [the cross]" (Colossians 2:9-15 AMP).

"To make all men see what is the fellowship of the mystery, which from the beginning of the world hath been hid in God, who created all things by

Jesus Christ: To the intent that now unto the principalities and powers in heavenly places might be known by the church the manifold wisdom of God, According to the eternal purpose which he purposed in Christ Jesus our Lord: In whom we have boldness and access with confidence by the faith of him" (Ephesians 3:9-12).

Words are clothes, transmitting spirit. How words are spoken will transmit the condition or the environment of that spirit. When we speak kindly, it is the spirit of kindness from the Holy Spirit that is being manifested. Happiness and joy are fruit of the Holy Spirit.

Depression, anger, and anxieties are fruit of demonic spirits. Medications can be given to treat the symptoms of these spirits, but they do not cause the spirit to leave the body. When we settle for maintaining or surviving a spiritual condition, we are living out of the Old Testament pattern of sins being covered by the shedding of animals' blood, but that does not get rid of it.

When God wants to deal with the essence, the victory over the situation, He does not just put a Band-Aid on it, dealing with it symptomatically. When a victory is manifested and a spirit is defeated, that negative spirit will be forced to flee, never to return to the presence of Christ in you. Someone around you can have demonic activity, but that activity will not come to you.

Whenever the Word of the Lord comes to us, it must go beyond the activity of religion that has our sins covered with the blood of the Lamb. *"For by your words you will be justified and acquitted, and by your words you will be condemned and sentenced"* (Matthew 12:37 AMP). The Word of the Lord must activate our conviction, an experience of exercising our faith.

Faith without works is dead. This is an intimate relationship with the Word of God and the Spirit of God in you. "The Spirit of God moves… God said…" (Genesis 1: 2-3).

"You believe that God is one; you do well. So do the demons believe and shudder [in terror and horror such as make a man's hair stand on end and contract the surface of his skin]! Are you willing to be shown [proof], you

foolish (unproductive, spiritually deficient) fellow, that faith apart from [good] works is inactive and ineffective and worthless?" (James 2:19-20 AMP).

Consider this example: Children are not produced by a couple sitting around their kitchen table, talking about having children. There must be a personal involved experience of intimacy. They can be joyful in the expectation and hope for a child to come forth as the fruit of their marriage, and they can have faith in believing that it is God's will for them to have children. However, without consummating the marriage, faith without experience of intimacy will not produce fruit.

It takes energy to put faith to work.

"The LORD thy God in the midst of thee (Christ in you) is mighty; he will save, he will rejoice over thee (you) with joy; he will rest (victory position/ silent satisfaction) in his love (identity/essence), he will joy over thee (you) with singing. I will gather them that are sorrowful (survival mode spirit) for the solemn assembly, who are of thee (cells of the body of Christ), to whom the reproach of it was a burden (could not see the finish victory). Behold, at that time I will undo all that afflict thee (you): and I will save her (the bride of Christ) that halted, and gather her that was driven out; and I will get them praise and fame in every land where they have been put to shame. At that time will I bring you again, even in the time that I gather you: for I will make you a name and praise among all people of the earth, when I turn back your captivity before your eyes, said the LORD" (Zephaniah 3:17-20).

God desires intimacy with His body in order to reach a silent, satisfactory rest of His bride overcoming the warfare within her. So that the fruit of His Holy Spirit will be produced in her innermost belly, removing the unwanted spirits of demonic influence. *"He who believes (experience intimacy) in Me [who cleaves to and trusts in and relies on Me] as the Scripture has said, From his innermost being shall flow [continuously] springs and rivers of living water. But He was speaking here of the Spirit, Whom those who believed (trusted, had faith) in Him were afterward to receive"* (John 7:38-39 AMP).

Once we come into that rest with Him, we enter into a season of miracles. True miracles are the result of an internal triumph. This is not just being healed from a sickness or disease, but acknowledging that your life is a miracle and you were created to live in a supernatural environment because your existence is in His image after His kind.

Religious Christianity will keep us in an environment where miracles are a magical encounter coming into a fallen man's world where he exists in a beastly/demonic domain. At a certain level of elementary beliefs there is a manifestation of supernatural power.

> **True miracles are the result of an internal triumph.**

Unfortunately, there is no assurance of the position and authority of living in the supernatural as an overcomer. As soon as a negative spirit tries to come back into the environment, religious Christians allow doubt and insecurity to question what God is doing. They bring logic and reason back into the realm where God established harmony and rest.

What we do not consider is that God desires to increase our faith. This comes about by our encounter with trials and tribulations. Are we dealing with these issues the same way we did before? Do we remember who we are in Christ and the power and authority He has given us?

For faith to be true it must be exercised

"Therefore, [inheriting] the promise (the revelation WORD given to you) is the outcome of faith and depends [entirely] on faith, in order that it might be given as an act of grace (unmerited favor), to make it stable and valid and guaranteed to all his descendants--not only to the devotees and adherents of the Law (religious Christians), but also to those who share the faith of Abraham, who is [thus] the father of us all. As it is written, I have made you the father of many nations. [He was appointed our father] in the sight of God in whom he believed, who gives life to the dead and speaks of the nonexistent things that [He has foretold and promised] as if they [already] existed. [For Abraham, human reason for] hope being gone, hoped in faith that he should become the father of many nations, as he had been promised, So [numberless] shall your descendants be" (Romans 4:16-18 AMP).

"WHEN ABRAM was ninety-nine years old, the Lord appeared to him and said, I am the Almighty God; walk and live habitually before Me and be perfect (blameless, wholehearted, complete)" (Genesis 17:1 AMP).

Here is some practical wisdom to help manifest the reality of being an overcomer:

For ninety-nine years Abram lived his life according to who he was in the identity of Abram. At this time we know that he had a relationship with God, was obedient to God, and conversed with God. In all aspects of what we would consider being a Christian today, Abram would qualify from an Old Testament perspective. He believed God and was counted as righteous.

Yet, it was while Abram was living out of his old name that God told him to walk before HIM and be perfect. This is not a position of being behind God and following HIM, or walking in front of God, but backwards. Abram walked before God with God at his back. Abram did not know where he was going or what his day would look like, but he knew that God had his back covered from any enemy that would try to accuse him. The only voice Abram could hear was God's, telling him to walk before Him in perfection.

This is FAITH!

How can we apply this to our own lives? Many of us use a day planner or a calendar to organize our schedules. I would suggest that you find a planner that would allow something to be written on it three or four lines each day. This is your planner with the Lord. Begin your day by writing a Scripture verse that God gives you on the first line. Then close your day planner and pray this verse to God, asking Him to show you what His WORD looks like for that day. At the end of the day, before going to bed, fill in the other lines with ONLY BLESSINGS that you received. Look for the simple things that you were blessed with: the cashier smiled at you in the grocery store, you had a few dollars to give to the homeless man on the corner, you made it to work on time with very little traffic issues, you weren't stranded in the bathroom because another family member didn't refill the toilet paper, this author just made you laugh when you felt like crying. Whatever simple blessings you received, and there had to be some because you are still alive and breathing, write down a few of them.

Each day, for six days, I would like to challenge you to practice this pattern. Then on the seventh day, do not seek God for another Scripture verse, but read the six days of blessings that you have written down over the past week. READ them out loud. READ them with passion and love, giving back to God the glory that He has crowned you with over the past week. This is the battle cry of victory that the people shouted after walking around Jericho for six days. This is the release of Abram becoming Abra -h-AM. The breath of God ("H") released in His temple, you and me as "AM", Christ in me.

Our Heavenly Father has covered our backs with His presence from our enemies (words and thoughts) of yesterday so that only His blessings can influence our today. Today, you are a new creation in Christ Jesus; the old man is gone and all things are new (2 Corinthians 5:17). Today, you are no longer living with the identity of the old Adam, but you have been quickened/changed by the Holy Spirit with the breath of God. You have been *"crucified with Christ: nevertheless you live; yet not as the old person covered with the blood of the Lamb, but Christ lives in you as you: and the life which you now live in the flesh you live by the faith of the Son of God, who loves you, and gave himself for you"*(Gal. 2:20).

"Then your light will break forth like the dawn, and your healing will quickly appear; then your righteousness will go before you, and the glory of the LORD will be your rear guard. Then you will call, and the LORD will answer; you will cry for help, and he will say: Here am I" (Isaiah 58:8-9 NIV).

Selah

Chapter 8

The NOW Moment:

Bringing the Eternal Presence of Christ into the Beautiful NOW

"Today, salvation, healing, and deliverance
has come to this house"
Luke 19:9 (NIV)

Today, we live at a time in history with the ability to capture our NOW moment using cameras, videos, and other media resources, bringing our past into present day. Have you ever noticed while looking through photos and reminiscing over past vacations, birthday parties, or family holidays that we tend to remember those moments with more intensity than when we were actually there?

We will often reflect on certain words that were spoken that made us feel good, or the smell of the air as we look at the pictures of the mountains. We can look at our pictures at the beach and hear the seagulls flying nearby, or the waves crashing on the shore.

What is amazing is that in the moment of actually experiencing the event, we rarely have the same intensity as when we recall it through pictures. The same effect is true in the Kingdom of God.

Today, we have the fullness of His Love, His Life, and the intensity of His presence, yet, it isn't until we move into another day and reflect on the event that we see His presence had always been with us.

> *Take your time to bring the eternal presence of Christ into your day by capturing the moments of acts of love that flow through you from heaven, and radiate to others.*

Those that have gone before us have the fullness of His presence, yet they cannot share this intensity with others because they too have the fullness of Christ Jesus. True Love must be shared with a servant's heart, unconditionally. For this reason, they surround us as a cloud of witnesses to encourage us to grasp the moment NOW and to bring the Kingdom of God into our present.

"There will be weeping and grinding of teeth when you see Abraham and Isaac and Jacob and all the prophets in the kingdom of God, but you yourselves being cast forth (banished, driven away)" (Luke 13:28 AMP).

Do not reminisce, wishing that you had captured the moment of God's Love in the intensity of the present moment. Take your time to bring the eternal presence of Christ into your day by capturing the moments with acts of love—giving a hug to a stranger, rejoicing at the laughter of a child playing, blessing a person with peace that is in a hurry, doing little things for others that will be appreciated, even without acknowledgement.

God is a consuming fire. His Word, His presence, is a lake of fire. If we allow the consuming fire of His presence to manifest the in the intensity of the moment, the pictures from our past will become our NOW, taking away the gnashing of teeth of tomorrow. The enemy of God wants to keep you enjoying the mundane goodness of life instead of capturing the full Excellency of His calling that is yours. The truth that exists is the domain of antichrist. There will be many Christians gnashing their teeth because they chose complacency of the moment rather than the full Kingdom NOW.

Selah

Chapter 9

Tabernacle Oneness

"The earth is the LORD's, and the fullness thereof; the world, and they that dwell therein."

Psalms 24:1 (KJV)

The season of Tabernacle Oneness.

"Thanks be to God, Who in Christ always leads us in triumph [as trophies of Christ's victory] and through us spreads and makes evident the fragrance of the knowledge of God everywhere, for we are the sweet fragrance of Christ [which exhales] unto God" (2 Corinthians 2:14-15a AMP).

These words of Paul describe an atmosphere that goes before us. It is a parade to celebrate the victory of our manifesting the glory of His presence in the world.

He goes on to say, *"For we are not as many, which corrupt the word of God: but as of sincerity, but as of God, in the sight of God speak we in Christ"* (vs. 17).

Notice Paul's words, "as of God, in the sight of God." These are not the words of a Christian that knows about God as a sinner saved by grace. They are not the wisdom of a Christian that fellowships with Christ having the ability to pray in tongues. Such positions are stepping stones for the preparation of the bride, but they have yet to encounter the experience of oneness with Christ as the beloved bridegroom.

The position that Paul is referring to is an experience that has already taken place by faith in Christ Jesus. This is a position of one that knows what it means to come boldly to the throne of God in the Holy of Holies. We no longer are coming to our Father as children with needs, but entering His presence as a prepared bride for her beloved bridegroom.

This is a position where God fellowships in intimate union to impregnate His seed with His own image and kind. His Holy Spirit quickens our own spirit as One (1 Corinthians 15:45). This experience requires a total surrender and death of the identity we had of yesterday (Galatians 2:20). The womb of His bride, His church, is to be the place where rivers of living water flows (John 7:38) to the heart of circumcision (Deuteronomy 30:6), then released by the mouth of His body (Matthew 15:8) filling the earth with His glory (Habakkuk 2:14).

This is a position where the Altar of Sacrifice is not only removing our sins. It is also our taking the blood covenant of Jesus Christ as a His bride, shedding our old name and nature. We have prepared ourselves as His spotless bride to enter into the Holy of Holies, willing to consummate the marriage with the Lamb of God. This is a personal experience with Jesus Christ that each member of His body must encounter. It is a Tabernacle experience of oneness.

Then corporately as one body, as His beloved wife, we exit the Holy of Holies with the testimony of blood covenant on our sheets and His fragrance of love upon on our hearts. The bride of Christ is only a bride for one day. After the marriage has been consummated by the Lamb of God, the church is the wife of Christ Jesus carrying His seed to reproduce His Kind. We have a responsibility to be His ambassador as king and priest reigning on the earth (Revelation 5:10).

When we come out through the veil and exit the inner court to be seen by the world we have a new name and nature in Christ Jesus as I AM (2 Corinthians 5:17). We have a responsibility while in our natural body to *"be fruitful, and multiply, and replenish the earth, and subdue it"* (Genesis 1:28). As His church/wife, we have the ability to carry His seed, the Word of God, in our inner most being to grow and develop. In the fullness of time, the birthing releases HIS WORD from our heart and fills the earth with God Kind. In this manner, *"The Word was made flesh, and dwelt among men, (and we beheld his glory, the glory as of the only begotten of the Father,) full of grace and truth"* (John 1:14). *"Behold the handmaid of the Lord; be it unto me according to thy word"* (Luke 1:38).

"The [Holy] Spirit and the bride (the church, the true Christians) say, Come!" (Revelation 22:17 AMP).

"The Spirit of God (Elohim, Christ) was moving (hovering, brooding) over the face of the waters (His beloved bride). And God said, Let there be light (Let there BE ME); and there was light" (Genesis 1:2b-3).

We as the body of Christ have the responsibility to fill the earth with the glory of the Lord that all creation groans to see manifested.

"This is the revelation of Jesus Christ [His unveiling of the divine mysteries]" (Revelation 1:1) *"I am the Alpha and the Omega, the First and the Last"* (Revelation 1:11 AMP)

As she leaves the Holy of Holies, she passes by the Altar of Incense, clothed with the sweet fragrance of the Lord, *"For God so loved, He gave…while we were still in darkness and sin"* (John 3:16, Romans 5:8). Her radiance of life is filled with the glory of her beloved. *"Now the Lord is the Spirit, and where the Spirit of the Lord is, there is liberty (emancipation from bondage, freedom). And all of us, as with unveiled face, [because we] continued to behold [in the Word of God] as in a mirror the glory of the Lord, are constantly being transfigured into His very own image in ever increasing splendor and from one degree of glory to another; [for this comes] from the Lord [Who is] the Spirit"* (2 Corinthians 3:17-18 AMP).

"The earth is the LORD's, and the fullness thereof; the world, and they that dwell therein" (Psalm 24:1).

It takes the position of being in Christ, one with Him as the head (Jesus Christ, Eph. 4:15) united with His body (the church, Romans 12:5) so that Christ is manifested in the earth as all and in all (Col. 3:11). *"For all who are led (gathered together in oneness in the Holy of Holies) by the Spirit of God are sons of God"* (Romans 8:14).

"For He has made known to us the mystery (secret) of His will (of His plan, of His purpose). [And it is this:] In accordance with His good pleasure (His merciful intention) which He had previously purposed and set forth in Him, [He planned] for the maturity of the times and the climax of the ages to unify all things and head them up and consummate them in Christ, [both] things in heaven and things on the earth" (Ephesians 1:9-10 AMP).

"I saw the Lord sitting upon a throne, high and lifted up, and the skirts of His train (His body, His wife) filled the [most holy part of the] temple… And one cried to another and said, Holy, holy, holy is the Lord of hosts; the whole earth is full of His glory!" (Isaiah 6:1, 3 AMP).

"The Lord said to me, Say not, I am only a youth (young bride); for you shall go to all to whom I shall send you, and whatever I command you, you shall speak. Be not afraid of them [their faces], for I am with you to deliver you, says the Lord. Then the Lord put forth His hand and touched my mouth. And the Lord said to me, Behold, I have put My words in your mouth. See, I have this day appointed you to the oversight of the nations and of the kingdoms to root out and pull down, to destroy and to overthrow, to build and to plant" (Jeremiah 1:7-10 AMP).

"May grace (God's unmerited favor) and spiritual peace [which means peace with God and harmony, unity, and undisturbedness] be yours from God our Father and from the Lord Jesus Christ. May blessing (praise, laudation, and eulogy) be to the God and Father of our Lord Jesus Christ (the Messiah) who has blessed us in Christ with every spiritual (given by the Holy Spirit) blessing in the heavenly realm! Even as [in His love] He chose us [actually picked us out for Himself as His own] in Christ before the foundation of the world, that we are holy (consecrated and set apart for Him) and blameless in His sight, even above reproach, before Him in love" (Ephesians 1:2-4 AMP).

Selah

Chapter 10

The End of Times is the Beginning of Christ:

Letting go of the Bridezilla mentality

"Those who live according to the flesh have their minds set on what the flesh desires; but those who live in accordance with the Spirit have their minds set on what the Spirit desires."
Romans 8:5

"I will give you a new heart and put a new spirit in you; I will remove from you your heart of stone and give you a heart of flesh."
Ezekiel 36:26

As I sit in my office knowing in my heart that there is a message I am to share through writing, I ponder seeking an unveiling of Christ that has not been heard. What are the keys to unlock the door of the mystery of Christ in you for the manifestation of the sons of God? I lean not to my own understanding, but to hear the Spirit of the Lord within me speaking His truth to share with His body.

In the Beginning… *"The earth* (me) *was without form, and void* (who am I)*; and darkness was upon the face* (identity) *of the deep* (my heart, inner most being). *And the Spirit of God moved* (impregnated, quickened) *upon the face of the waters* (the seed of God planted as my DNA). *And God* (Christ) *said, Let there be light* (god, me): *and there was light* (birthing of His seed). *And God* (Christ) *saw the light* (His son), *that it was good: and God* (Christ) *divided the light* (identity in Him) *from the darkness* (ignorance, unknown)" (Genesis 1:2-3).

For those that have been following the lessons that I have shared over the past several years, you will recall a pattern that has been emerging to *"Bring forth the sons of God"* and about *"Living in the Inheritance of God,"* our Father, as new creations in Christ Jesus. I have also been given the assignment by the Holy Spirit to dissect the Book of Revelation verse by verse, unveiling the finished work of Jesus Christ as *"Christ in you, the hope of glory."* This is still a work in progress, but the Lord has taken me to the end of Revelation (Chapter 22) to give me insight on "end times."

"The Spirit and the bride say, Come. And let him that heareth say, Come. And let him that is athirst come. And whosoever will, let him take the water of life freely" (Revelation 22:17).

For over 2,000 years, the church has taught that they are the "bride of Christ" spoken of in Revelation 22:17. However, the reason the church is still teaching of a coming bridegroom instead of living today as new creations in Christ (Gal. 2:20), is because they are stuck in the preparation stage of planning their wedding. The church today is still a display of being a "bridezilla" preparing for a coming wedding with a man that they are not sure if he is white, black, yellow, or red-skinned.

Does He have blue, black, or brown eyes? Is He still hanging on the cross, covered in blood that is over 2,000 years old, or is He clothed as a Greek god that can walk through walls?

What do I mean when I use the word "bridezilla?" If you have ever been involved with helping a bride-to-be put together her wedding, then you would have a concept of what it means to be a "bridezilla." Most wedding planner books suggest that a time span of eight months to a year be set aside for arranging a wedding.

During the initial stage of preparation there is a lot of excitement and energy between the bride and those that are helping. Many ideas and thoughts are being shared. Many decisions are being made. The bride initially is open to these suggestions as she incorporates her own ideas, but she is also very in tune to the fact that this is her wedding. A bride considers that she is only going to have one opportunity in her life to have the wedding of her dreams, and when the wedding is over, she won't have any more moments. With that pressure being around a bride-to-be, before the wedding and all the way up until she is standing at the altar, can be a very trying experience for anyone connected with the preparation. This is when the word "bridezilla" is formed.

Everything is centered and focused on the BRIDE. It is one of the most glorious and self-centered moments of a woman's life. Many women consider this the peak of a woman's glory and radiance. It is a time in her life when all eyes and attention are focused on her, including the groom. She knows in her heart that every hair must be in place. Her make-up must be flawless. Her nails must be perfectly manicured and polished. The pearls on her dress must lay in such an array that gives her an hourglass figure. The folds in her veil must be layered, giving her a crown of glory. Her bouquet must be perfectly arranged, giving off the fragrance of elegance as a princess walking between the people in her world.

There have been many relationships severed after the wedding is over because of the "bridezilla" being manifested while preparations for the wedding took place. Many brides spend the majority of their energy focused on the wedding day, but very little energy about their new life, no longer as a bride, but a wife.

Not only does the church display a "bridezilla" mentality to the world, but the church does not agree of who they are supposed to be marrying for eternity. Over all, the many different denominations of Christianity say they "love the Lord Jesus Christ," but if the question arises to describe Him, the groom, each Christian has a different description based on their imagination of who Jesus Christ is today.

Would we dare to tell the "bridezilla" church that the only wedding they are preparing for is in their imagination? If that isn't enough to think about, do we even try to ask, "So, what happens after the wedding with Jesus Christ?" Do you plan on living in a mansion in the sky surrounded with streets of gold? Do you have visions of a perfectly formed fleshly body with not an ounce of fat that never gets older than "30?" Will that flesh have smooth silky skin with no wrinkles and topped with a head full of long, flowing, radiant hair?

WAKE UP CHURCH! As long as the church gives this imaginative picture of what it means to be the bride of Christ married to a picture of a man that an artist has illustrated of Jesus, we are living in the world of imagination as children of God, instead of sons.

Jesus Christ brought the creation of heaven and earth together (Genesis 1:1) when He died on the cross, descended into the depth of hell (ignorance and darkness), and ascended to the throne room of God, bringing all of mankind with Him. He unlocked, exposed, and overcame every form of ignorance and darkness that could control and rob mankind from the ability to be who they were created to be in Christ, taking us back to the beginning of creation. The tomb where the body of Jesus Christ was laid was found empty and void of any flesh or bones. So why does the bride of Christ, the church, keep hanging around the cross waiting for her knight in shining armor?

The church has been trying to figure out "who they are" being tossed to and fro justifying the means of how to prepare themselves without spot or wrinkle to be the bride of Christ from the interpretation of men. Men can talk to women about how to be a bride and how to have a child, but without the experience, there is no reality. Do we really desire for the return of the Lord, or do we just want to talk about our imagination of what we "think" the end of times and the coming of the Lord is about?

"All power is given unto me in heaven and in earth. Go ye therefore, and teach all nations, baptizing them in the name of the Father, and of the Son, and of the Holy Ghost: Teaching them to observe all things whatsoever I have commanded you: and, lo, I am with you always, even unto the end of the world. Amen." (Matthew 28:18-20).

Selah

Chapter 11

Love Casts out Fear

"There is no fear in love. But perfect love drives out fear, because fear has to do with punishment. The one who fears is not made perfect in love."

1 John 4:17-18 (NIV)

*T*here is no fear in love, in God, and nothing is impossible for Him.

"Peace I leave with you; my peace I give you. I do not give to you as the world gives. Do not let your hearts be troubled and do not be afraid" (John 14:27 NIV).

Jesus gave us his peace that surpasses all of our natural understanding, telling us that God is love. It is with His identity in His heart located within each of us that all fears of our imagination and tormenting voices must flee (1 John 4:16). Our Heavenly Father is a jealous Dad who will not allow any idols (fears) in His house (you). Even the power to remove the "tormenting fears" we struggle with daily belongs to God (Psalm 62:11).

How many deceptive voices are counseling your mind? The fear of:

- Death
- Loss of job
- Change
- What others think
- What is happening with my children
- Concern with family or friends
- Darkness
- Health
- Insecurity
- Being a sinner or doing something wrong
- Lack of finances
- Falsely judged
- Insecurity
- Correction
- Loss of control
- _____ (fill in the blank)

We have not received the spirit of bondage to these or any other fears, but we have received the Spirit of God, allowing us to boldly go before the throne of God and call Him Father (Romans 8:15). God did not give us the spirit of fear; but of power, and of love, and of a righteous mind (2 Timothy 1:7).

The reason these fears enter our thoughts is not that God wants to condemn us, for there is no condemnation in Christ Jesus who gave us the Spirit of Life and Power. God has allowed these counselors of "fear" to come forth into the light of our awareness (His presence within us) so that the thoughts of our imagination are judged within ourselves, allowing the perfect love we have in Him to cast out all our fears.

Paul says 1 Corinthians 4:3-5, *"I care very little if I am judged by you or by any human court; indeed, I do not even judge myself. My conscience is clear, but that does not make me innocent. The Lord judges me. Therefore, judge nothing before the appointed time; wait till the Lord comes. He will bring to light what is hidden in darkness and will expose the motives of men's hearts. At that time each will receive his praise from God"* (NIV).

God has allowed your fears and thoughts of the imagination to come forth so that He can reveal Christ within you. The kingdom of God is righteousness, peace, and joy in the Holy Spirit. It is not just in word, but also in His power that we manifest His presence through our faith in God.

We are not to be afraid or tormented when our thoughts or imagination try to counsel us with "fear," but to have faith in God that it is our Father's good pleasure to give us His kingdom, today (Luke 12:32).

It is with this understanding that our love, our identity in Christ, is made perfect.

God's perfect love in you will cast out all imagination of fearful thoughts, making them perfect in His love. Bring your concerns and fears before the Lord, allowing Him to remove them as He surrounds you with His peace. We understand the reason that we were made aware of any fear is so that His presence, His love, His life, within us can cast out those "fears," allowing our identity in Christ to be made perfect.

It is in this perfection that when others see us, they see their Heavenly Father…for it is Christ in us, the hope of His glory, which is manifested in the earth as the sons of God.

"Praise be to the God and Father of our Lord Jesus Christ! In his great mercy he has given us new birth into a living hope through the resurrection of Jesus Christ from the dead, and into an inheritance that can never perish, spoil or fade-kept in heaven for you, who through faith are shielded by God's power until the coming of the salvation that is ready to be revealed in the last time. In this you greatly rejoice, though now for a little while you may have had to suffer grief in all kinds of trials. These have come so that your faith-of greater worth than gold, which perishes even though refined by fire-may be proved genuine and may result in praise, glory and honor when Jesus Christ is revealed. Though you have not seen him, you love him; and even though you do not see him now, you believe in him and are filled with an inexpressible and glorious joy, for you are receiving the goal of your faith, the salvation of your souls" (1 Peter 1:3-9 NIV).

Selah

Chapter 12

Reigning Through Prayer:

Applying Ezekiel's prayer

"I will sprinkle clean water on you, and you will be clean;
I will cleanse you from all your impurities and from all your idols.
I will give you a new heart and put a new spirit in you;
I will remove from you your heart of stone and give
you a heart of flesh. And I will put my Spirit in you and move
you to follow my decrees and be careful to keep my laws."

Ezekiel 36:25-27 (NIV)

*G*od gave the vision of the valley of dry bones to his prophet Jeremiah because his heart weeps over the dry bones of his people, as Jesus wept over the city of Jerusalem. The Spirit of God desires to breathe new life into vast areas of spiritual dryness, barrenness, and deadness. I identified with the need of that family and prayed for that young life through Ezekiel's picture in Ezekiel 37.

This passage can be intensely personal. Take strength and comfort from these prayers. Re-center yourself on God's purposes and promises, and take up new, prayer weapons to fight the real enemy, not the person. Ask for a weeping heart of mercy, not judgment, to carry the gift of discernment for repentance. Until you can put your tears and your life on the line for the person, marriage, family, church, city, or nation, you do not have the heart and mind of Jesus for them. Open your Bible to Ezekiel 37 and read, crying out to God for your own "dry bones" situations in your family.

Ezekiel 37:

37:1 Father, your hand is upon us in Spirit-led intercession for_____. Purify our hearts by your Spirit and deposit your burden of prayer in us, unmixed with unsanctified sympathies, anger, bitterness, or human judgments. We are trusting you to bring us through the valley of the shadow of death, as you promised. Lead us to pray as large, deep, and wide as your providence in this situation. Give us a heart of wisdom and mercy that rejoices against judgment for_____.

37:2 We trust that you have gone before and are working, even when we don't see your purposes. Spirit of the Lord, lead us to rightly discern the real condition of_____, not just react to what we think or have been told. You see the dry bones of barrenness and desolation. You know the entrances that _____has given the kingdom of evil.

is oppressed, fragmented, miserable and unhappy, alienated from your blessing, morally compromised with sin and deception, rebelling against their parents and your Word, and in great danger. Their present condition is not hopeless to you. In darkness, you are light.

37:3 Spirit of counsel, you know everything. You don't need us to inform you. You want from us restful, trusting communion and absolute surrender to your will, your ways, and your timing. We humbly acknowledge our total dependence on you for faith to stand, for knowledge and counsel, for comfort and security, for direction and outcome. Let us speak only your prayers. Let us not accept as final the circumstances of evil and iniquity that our eyes see. You alone know the end from the beginning, and you are the God of the impossible.

37:4 Say to deaf ears, "Hear the word of the Lord!" At your direction, let us discern and pray your purposes for_____ and the entire family. Speak your words to them and cause them to respond obediently to you. Enable us to pray your prayers for the dry bones of_____'s body and soul (heart, mind, will, and emotions). Holy Spirit, call forth your purposes and the future and hope that you have planned for_____.

37:5-6 Sovereign Lord, speak your creative and restoring miracle to _____ 's life with the same resurrection power that brought Jesus to life from the dead. Breathe new life into them by your Spirit. Set everything in place in your order in their life, so that_____will know that you are Lord, Sovereign Ruler, rightfully due their loyalty and obedient service.

37:7 By faith, we believe you, obey you, and pray as you command. Answer by your Spirit and open a way where there seems to be no way. You go before, for you are the God of break-through. Give us a sign of encouragement. Let us hear the "rattling bones" coming together as you make _____who you intend them to be: healthy, whole, functioning, life-giving. By your blood, Lord Jesus, regenerate life in them and cause the marrow of their inner being to begin to sustain life.

37:8 Thank you for every sign of Your goodness we see, no matter how small. You are answering, and we ask you to do it thoroughly. Superficial answers, cleaning up their act, and looking functional are not enough! Stop short of nothing less than a new heart, a new spirit, a new life. Enable us to reach deeper into your heart to pray your promises until your full purposes are accomplished in all the family.

37:9 Sovereign Lord, call forth from the north, the south, the east, and the west the breath of life for_____. You formed them in their mother's womb, and as you breathed in them the first breath of their life, breathe into them the new life of the Spirit in all your favor and purpose. Restore them to wholeness. Speak to them, "Choose wisdom, choose righteousness, choose freedom, and choose life!"

37:10-11 No situation is hopeless to you. Sovereign Lord, break off the shackles of captivity. Cause_____to stand up in all the fullness of your redeeming power. Make_____mighty in your Spirit. Deliver them as an effectual weapon in your hand. Set into them your spiritual gifts and calling among their generation of yet-to-be evangelists, preachers, disciples, and world-changers that Satan is working overtime to annihilate. Let us see your glory in these things that were intended for evil.

37:12 You have the keys to open the prison doors of sin, bondage, and destruction. Bring this captive out into all their true inheritance in you. Restore them to the family and the family of God.

37:13-14 Father, act in such a way that_____'s transformation will be a testimony to your redemptive power. What you are doing, do quickly. In Jesus' name, Amen.

Chapter 13

What Are You Doing?

Observing yourself daily with the actions and attitude of Christ

---

"Brothers and sisters, I could not address you as people who live by the Spirit but as people who are still worldly—mere infants in Christ. I gave you milk, not solid food, for you were not yet ready for it. Indeed, you are still not ready. You are still worldly. For since there is jealousy and quarreling among you, are you not worldly? Are you not acting like mere humans?"

1 Corinthians 3:1-3 (NIV)

*W*e have permission and authority today to move and function on this earth as kings/queens and priests in this world (1 John 4:17).

"Entering into this fullness is not something you figure out or achieve. It's not a matter of being circumcised or keeping a long list of laws. No, you're already in—insiders—not through some secretive initiation rite but rather through what Christ has already gone through for you, destroying the power of sin. If it's an initiation ritual you're after, you've already been through it by submitting to baptism. Going under the water was a burial of your old life; coming up out of it was a resurrection, God raising you from the dead as he did Christ. When you were stuck in your old sin-dead life, you were incapable of responding to God. God brought you alive—right along with Christ! Think of it! All sins forgiven, the slate wiped clean, that old arrest warrant canceled and nailed to Christ's cross." (Colossians 2:11-15 Msg)

"If you're serious about living this new resurrection life with Christ, act like it. Pursue the things over which Christ presides. Don't shuffle along, eyes to the ground, absorbed with the things right in front of you. Look up, and be alert to what is going on around Christ—that's where the action is. See things from his perspective. Your old life is dead. Your new life, which is your real life—even though invisible to spectators— is with Christ in God. He is your life." (Colossians 3:1-3 Msg)

Christians have the elevated status to perceive and understand situations from a heavenly position versus the logic and reasoning that most of humanity does. We are supposed to be living, thinking, and making decisions to move forward from our height in heaven. Paul tells the church in Philippi, *"I press on toward the goal to win the [supreme and heavenly] prize to which God in Christ Jesus is calling us upward."* (Phil. 3:14 AMP).

So what keeps us from ruling and reigning from our inheritance we already have in heaven? First, we must know who we are in Christ. Then, from that position in oneness with Him, the decree and scepter

He has given us releases His Love and joy into the midst of the trials and tribulations.

Often, we love with intensity and passion, weeping as we see, or come to know about crisis issues in someone's life. It is a natural response of our soul and emotions. When I did my pastoral counseling training as a chaplain at a local hospital, I was constantly in an atmosphere of family and friends overwhelmed with the acute suddenness of dealing with life and death issues. The crossroads of shock and denial would instantly take over the atmosphere. My purpose was to present a "calming presence" according to the hospital rules, but I would often find myself asking Papa God, "What would Jesus be doing right now? Would He heal all and raise the dead? Would He do nothing but simply BE there and let the circumstance dictate the future? How would Jesus find joy in the midst of death?"

It's easy to preach about rising up higher into the heavens if you go into your prayer closet, fast, read Scriptures, declare the WORD, have more faith, praise the Lord, etc. However, when you're on the front line of a life and death battle and the enemy is ready to kill you, do you start screaming Scriptures and singing praises with faith and boldness that you can't die?

I'm not preaching, I'm asking. What would the Jesus you know do that would be different from what you're doing when confronted suddenly with life and death? What was going on inside Paul to write, *"Your old life is dead and you are NOW living the resurrected Life of Christ Jesus?"* (2 Corinth 15).

Selah

Chapter 14

The Sign of Your Coming

"There is therefore now no condemnation to them which are in Christ Jesus, who walk not after the flesh, but after the Spirit."

Romans 8:1 (KJV)

The mystery Jesus shares of the end times is that there will be many that have a great calling on their life to be in ministry; however, they will not be teaching and preaching according to what God has orchestrated. But since they have the gift and the anointing of God, signs and wonders will be seen.

"Then if any man shall say unto you, Lo, here is Christ, or there; believe it not. For there shall arise false Christs, and false prophets, and shall shew great signs and wonders; insomuch that, if it were possible, they shall deceive the very elect. Behold, I have told you before" (Matthew. 24:23-25).

This famous chapter in Matthew is often taught by pastors as the "signs" that the end of time is near. Jesus tells us that there will be those that are anointed with the gifts of God where signs and wonders will follow. Since God gives the gifts and does not take them back, we have a key to understanding a mystery that Jesus is sharing about the coming of the Lord.

Jesus is telling us that it is possible for an anointed one of God, **the very elect** (apostle, prophet, pastor, teacher, or evangelist) to teach and prophesy opposition of what God has called for them to share. They are holding an incorrect stance of what God has called them to unveil to the body of Christ. The elect are those teaching the Scriptures partially, but interpreting them as if it is the fullness of the Father's thoughts. As a result, we have the building of doctrines and theologies created through partiality instead of the fullness of the Holy Spirit.

Jesus calls them "false christs and false prophets" with a false anointing. I repeat, Jesus is telling us that it will be possible for the elect of God, those that have a calling on their life by God to be deceived, teaching falseness that God did not anoint them with. Some will have power in their ministry, attracting crowds, but God says it is against what He called them to share. Some will even have the demonstration of the glory of God but not the truth of the glory.

Until one has been purified by the trials and tribulations in the valley of the shadow of death (the battle of Armageddon in the mind) and resurrected to know the fullness of God's love and peace while in the midst of the battle, one cannot give away the resurrected life of Christ Jesus.

God's love is a consuming fire. We either receive it, becoming transformed into His image, or we become consumed.

The enquiry of the disciples in Matthew 24 was about the coming of the Lord. What is the sign? The body of Christ Jesus. The bride that He is coming for must be purified with the character and nature of God (symbolized as gold without spot or wrinkle). Again, there will be those that have an anointing on their life by God, teaching purification of the bride according to their doctrine, showing signs and wonders, but Jesus says they are false prophets. **This is a sign of the end of the age we are in. This does not mean the end of the world, but the end of the system as we know it of how the church—the bride of Christ—is to be purified.**

The church of the Lord Jesus Christ, His body, is not a gender issue for male interpretation. It is an equality of male and female created in the image of God, both referred to as Adam (Genesis 5:1-2). The purification of the body of Christ is a blood issue. The cleansing of the bride of Christ without spot or wrinkle can only be grasped from the blood cleansing that women endure monthly and that is connected to LIFE. Until the elect recognize the spiritual balance of God's image as male and female in His creation, they will be deceived.

Another issue that must be taken into consideration as we consider the end of time is that all the parts of the body of Christ are in heaven and earth. One person is not the whole body of Christ. If we only focus on ourselves (will I be raptured out before the world comes to an end; will I go to heaven), then the enemy of God is winning the battle of Armageddon taking place within us.

The body of Christ is not just one person, one local church building, one particular denomination, one theological understanding, or even one country. If people in another

We cannot give to others what we do not believe within ourselves.

country are hurting and being persecuted for the gospel, then the other parts of the body in other parts of heaven and earth will be affected. If my little toe on my right foot was bruised, it would affect my whole body. I would be focused on how I would be able to walk, what shoes I could wear, whether I needed to prop my foot up or bandage it, etc. My thoughts throughout my day would constantly be redirected to my bruised toe because it hurts. This is how we need to understand the fullness of the body of the Lord Jesus Christ around the world; male and female; young and old.

As a little girl, I can remember being told to clean my plate because there were children in other parts of the world that were starving, and I should be thankful that I had food. Trying to be an obedient child, I would clean my plate not questioning how overeating was going to affect starving children in other countries.

Today, I can affect those children in other countries by giving them bone of my bone and flesh of my flesh in Christ Jesus. *"Jesus said, I have food (nourishment) to eat of which you know nothing and have no idea"* (John 4:32 AMP). Jesus' disciples did not understand the food that gives life.

We are at a time in history that has never been seen before where we can connect with parts of the body of Christ instantly around the world while sitting in our own home. We can pray and bless other members of the body, feeding them a meal from our Heavenly Father's table while we are walking in a park via cell phones, computers, and texting. In the twinkling of an eye, we have the power and capability of our Heavenly Father to bring the resurrected life of Christ to the body, filling the earth with the glory of God.

The famous "rapture sermons" that have been taught by the elect from 1 Thessalonians 4 and 5 are taking place today. However, since many are interpreting these Scriptures according to doctrine and theology, they are being deceived as Christians.

To begin understanding the signs of the coming of the Lord, the mature in Christ, male and female, must be in a correct position as kings and priests unto the Lord. This is why intercession and prayers of the righteous are so important.

"They sung a new song, saying, Thou art worthy to take the book, and to open the seals thereof: for thou was slain, and hast redeemed us to God by thy blood out of every kindred, and tongue, and people, and nation; And hast made us unto our God kings and priests: and we shall reign on the earth" (Rev. 5: 9-10).

God says, *"As He is, so are you in this world"* (1 John 4:17). The natural gives us discernment of what the body of Christ needs, but if we only take care of the natural issues, then we are not allowing the body of Christ to be healed with the fullness of the life of Jesus Christ. We must first align ourselves with the heavenly body of Christ so that we can see and understand the natural issues from God's perspective to bring transformation of the whole spotless bride of Christ into manifestation.

The end of time as we know it is now. With the power of cyberspace networking, the body of Christ has the ability to bring to manifestation the coming of the Lord and fill the earth with the glory of God. In the twinkle of an eye we can win the battle of Armageddon whose captain is "self" being controlled by the spirit of fear for the sake of looking out for "number one."

The time is now to allow Jesus Christ to be our captain putting on the Spirit of faith and allowing *"the fruit of the [Holy] Spirit [the work which His presence within accomplishes] of love, joy (gladness), peace, patience (an even temper, forbearance), kindness, goodness (benevolence), faithfulness, gentleness (meekness, humility), self-control (self-restraint, continence). Against such things there is no law [that can bring a charge]. And those who belong to Christ Jesus (the Messiah) have crucified the flesh (the godless human nature) with its passions and appetites*

> **The time is now for the coming of the Lord to be manifested in this world.**

and desires. If we live by the [Holy] Spirit, let us also walk by the Spirit. [If by the Holy Spirit we have our life in God,

let us go forward walking in line, our conduct controlled by the Spirit.]" (Galatians 5:22-25 AMP).

There is a company of people today around the world that are filled with the Holy Spirit knowing they are a member of the resurrected body of Christ Jesus. They are ready to lay down their carnal life and unite His body in this earth by His faith, transforming the atmosphere of fear into the glory of God.

Are you one of those people? Then arise and shine where God has planted you today. Your light, Christ in you the hope of glory has come (Isaiah 60). *"You are the light of the world* (the world that you are planted)"(Matthew 5:14). Fill your atmosphere with His love, grace, and mercy because He loved you first while you were still in darkness and ignorance. *"Seek first the kingdom of God and His righteousness"* (Matthew 6:33). *"Trust in the Lord with all your heart and lean not on your own understanding; in all your ways acknowledge him, and he will make your paths straight"* (Proverbs 3:5-6).

The Holy Spirit will equip us to do the Father's business as a son of God because we are connected to His glorious resurrected body. Today is the day to utilize the gifts and talents that He has instilled in each of us for such a time as this to be released in the earth. Today, there is no condemnation in Christ Jesus (Romans 8:1).

"Since Christ is in you, your body (old nature, ego) *is dead because of sin, yet your spirit is alive because of righteousness. Since the Spirit of him who raised Jesus from the dead is living in you, he who raised Christ from the dead will also give life to your mortal bodies through his Spirit, who lives in you"* (Romans 8:10- 11).

The greatest opposition existing today to the body of the resurrected life of Christ Jesus is the religious system of the church. The children of God are living in bondage of doctrines and traditions calling it the life of being a disciple of Christ, yet, being far removed from living in their inheritance as new creations in Christ as the resurrected body of Christ Jesus. This is a repeat of history when Jesus walked the earth. It was not the Gentile religions that Jesus had to stand against, but those that knew the Scriptures, but did not know the love and mercy that goes before judgment and condemnation.

Jesus came to set the captive heart free. As part of His body, is this your heart?

Selah

Chapter 15

The Preeminence of Christ

The Peace of Omnipresence and His
Fullness that is ALL in ALL

"For in Christ all the fullness of the Deity lives
in bodily form, and in Christ you have been
brought to fullness. He is the head
over every power and authority."

Colossians 2:9-10

"Thus it is written, the first man Adam became a living being (an individual personality); the last Adam (Christ) became a life-giving Spirit [restoring the dead to life]" (1 Corinthians 15:45 AMP). Adam was born again! Since Christ Jesus, the last Adam died and rose again from the dead to life, He brought total restoration to the Adam image that was created in the image of the Father. Jesus told Mary, "Touch me not; for I am not yet ascended to my Father: but go to my brethren, and say unto them, I ascend unto my Father, and your Father; and to my God, and your God." (John 20:17).

When we were first born in the flesh as a baby, our spirit, soul, and body came into this world through a Tabernacle, open heaven encounter from eternity into time. We were so familiar with the connection of our identity as spirit that we did not have any concept of time, sorrow, punishment, or death. All we understood was LIFE, JOY, and PEACE. Everything was good, filled with LIFE, and alive. Death was not an existence to our understanding. We came out of a life realm, so all we knew was LIFE. It wasn't until we learned the boundaries that time placed within our realm that we began to learn the opposites of good and evil. Our dog dies; we lose our favorite blanket; our favorite toy is broken or stops working, etc. We become exposed to learn that there is another tree called Knowledge in the midst of our garden, where we have been surrounded by LIFE.

As we grew and developed in our soul, we began to take on more understanding of our surroundings in time versus the LIFE of our identity as a spirit being of God. We developed pressures and anxieties that were not born with us, but were drawing us to search out our purpose and lead us to God. We come to an "age of accountability," according to many theologians, which is a Passover experience, to relearn who we are in Christ. Yet we are now being taught with the legalism of the church or the body of Christ versus the mind of Christ (Spirit) that has been filtered through heaven and hell concepts (the Tree of Knowledge). We come to know Jesus Christ as our Passover Lamb who died for our sins and was resurrected from the dead three days later.

Then approximately nine months later, we celebrate the adult Son of God who is seated with the Father, only to come back to earth again as a baby. This becomes the extent of most believers in Christ.

The body can only help carry you through time until death occurs, allowing the LIFE of Christ in Spirit and Truth to rule and reign over you.

Galatians 2:20:

"I have been crucified with Christ [in Him I have shared His crucifixion]; it is no longer I who live, but Christ (the Messiah) lives in me; and the life I now live in the body I live by faith in (by adherence to and reliance on and complete trust in) the Son of God, Who loved me and gave Himself up for me." (AMP)

God provides us with His faith and His Word, Jesus Christ, to counter balance the things we learn of this world and to bring us back into our true identity as spirit. We are now coming to the Father, not as a child, but one that is grown up in His LOVE and identity, recognizing in faith the family that we belong to while in this world. A child-like faith is innocent (ignorance), but the faith of a son, as Paul shares in Gal. 2:20, is the awakening into the faith of Holiness. Once there is a point of making choices in our experiences, we choose whether or not to come into our Father's Kingdom out of faith instead of innocence. This is the call of a son, ready to do the Father's business for the Father to be glorified only, not for the reward of the son.

We are NOW able to make "Holy Choices" that align with our original state as being a "son of God" (Galatians 3:26) in Spirit and Truth (John 4:23) with the image, likeness, character, and nature (Genesis 1:27) of our Heavenly Father with the mind of Christ (1 Corinthians 2:16) that declares that As HE IS, SO AM I in this world today (1 John 4:17). This becomes our personal Pentecost experience.

After you have suffered a little while…

1 Peter 5:10-11 (AMP*), "And after you have suffered a little while, the God of all grace [Who imparts all blessing and favor], Who has called you to His [own] eternal glory in Christ Jesus, will Himself complete and make you what you ought to be, establish and ground you securely, and strengthen, and settle you. To Him be the dominion (power, authority, rule) forever and ever. Amen (so be it)."*

God has always searched through the crowds in every generation to apprehend a first-fruits remnant people that will be of His kind, His resemblance. These are not your common people preaching and sharing God's word, declaring themselves Christians. The simple-minded Christian considers every believer to be equal, but the truth is that God has not called equality for His sovereign purpose, but has designed a destiny in each of us for His divine will to be manifested. Our purpose has been formed in God. He has chosen and not chosen to carry through His purpose.

Example: God chose Jacob, a schemer, not the firstborn twin Esau, to carry through His divine plan (Abraham, Isaac, and Jacob. Joseph (Jesus). God did not love Jacob more than Esau, but God had a purpose, a destiny of choice that Esau had no say so about.

When God gives us a map in the Old Testament of His temple, specifying that there are three courts—outer (elementary), middle (wisdom), and inner (transformation)—He is showing us a pattern design of His purpose. In every tabernacle or temple that God has built, the outer court is wide to include much, but when you come into the middle court of wisdom it is smaller and different than the outer court. There is a remnant that God has chosen that is qualified to enter into the Holy of Holies or the inner court; it is very small with very strict standards required for entry or else death comes upon you. There is entrance into the Holy of Holies while in the natural body, but there must be death of your identity which takes place first in the other two courts allowing the MIND of CHRIST to rule and reign.

Luke 1: 35 AMP, *"Then the angel said to her, The Holy Spirit will come upon you, and the power of the Most High will overshadow you [like a* shining cloud]; and so the holy (pure, sinless) Thing (Offspring) which shall be born of you will be called the Son of God."*

Colossians 1:27 AMP, *"To whom God was pleased to make known how great for the Gentiles are the riches of the glory of this mystery, which is Christ within and among you, the Hope of [realizing the] glory."*

Luke 1:37 AMP, *"For with God nothing is ever impossible and no word from God shall be without power or impossible of fulfillment."*

The shepherds in the field (earth bound) were seeking a savior for themselves.

Luke 2:8-9, *"And in that vicinity there were shepherds living [out under the open sky] in the field, watching [in shifts] over their flock by night. And behold, an angel of the Lord stood by them, and the glory of the Lord (sons of God) flashed and shone all about them, and they were terribly frightened."* Luke 2:15, *"When the angels (messengers/sons of God) went away from them into heaven, the shepherds said one to another, Let us go over to Bethlehem and see this thing (saying) that has come to pass, which the Lord has made known to us."*

The wise men (heaven bound) from the east brought gifts as they sought a KING for the kings/lords.

Matthew 2:2, *"Where is He who has been born King of the Jews? For we have seen His star in the east at its rising and have come to worship Him)."* These are the outer court and middle court people in the temple of God.

This remnant of people that God has chosen to enter into His high calling takes place through Christ Jesus. *"Jesus saith unto him, I am the way, the truth, and the life: no man cometh unto the Father, but by me"* (John 14:6). This does not mean they are "better" or "holier than thou," but that God has placed a unique anointing on their life that separates them from those that dwell in the outer and middle courts. There is something about them that is different and out of the ordinary from those that dwell in the realm of salvation or gifts of the Holy Spirit.

Romans 11: 1-8 KJV:

"I say then, hath God cast away his people? God forbid. For I also am an Israelite, of the seed of Abraham, of the tribe of Benjamin. God hath not cast away his people which he foreknew. Know you not what the scripture saith of Elias? How he maketh intercession to God against Israel saying, Lord, they have killed thy prophets, and digged down thine altars; and I am left alone, and they seek my life. But what saith the answer of God unto him? I have reserved to myself seven thousand men, who have not bowed the knee to the image of Baal (image of confusion, the image of ignorance).*Even so then at this present time also there is a remnant according to the election of grace.*

And if by grace, then is it no more of works: otherwise grace is no more grace. But if it be of works, then it is no more grace: otherwise work is no more work. What then? Israel hath not obtained that which he seeketh for; but the election hath obtained it and the rest were blinded. (According as it is written, God hath given them the spirit of slumber, eyes that they should not see, and ears that they should not hear;) unto this day."

Romans 11:2-5 AMP:

"No, God has not rejected and disowned His people [whose destiny] He had marked out and appointed and foreknown from the beginning. Do you not know what the Scripture says of Elijah, how he pleads with God against Israel? Lord, they have killed your prophets; they have demolished your altars, and I alone am left, and they seek my life. But what is God's reply to him? I have kept for Myself seven thousand men who have not bowed the knee to Baal! So too at the present time, there is a remnant (a small believing minority), selected (chosen) by grace (by God's unmerited favor and graciousness)."

Ephesians 1: 4-12 AMP:

"Even as [in His love] He chose us [actually picked us out for Himself as His own] in Christ before the foundation of the world, that we should be holy (consecrated and set apart for Him) and blameless in His sight, even above reproach, before Him in love. For He foreordained us (destined us,

planned in love for us) to be adopted (revealed) as His own children through Jesus Christ, in accordance with the purpose of His will because it pleased Him and was His kind intent] [So that we might be] to the praise and the commendation of His glorious grace (favor and mercy), which He so freely bestowed on us in the Beloved. In Him we have redemption (deliverance and salvation) through His blood, the remission (forgiveness) of our offenses (shortcomings and trespasses), in accordance with the riches and the generosity of His gracious favor, which He lavished upon us in every kind of wisdom and understanding (practical insight and prudence), making known to us the mystery (secret) of His will (of His plan, of His purpose). [And it is this:] In accordance with His good pleasure (His merciful intention) which He had previously purposed and set forth in Him, [He planned] for the maturity of the times and the climax of the ages to unify all things and head them up and consummate them in Christ, [both] things in heaven and things on the earth. In Him we also were made [God's] heritage (portion) and we obtained an inheritance; for we had been foreordained (chosen and appointed beforehand) in accordance with His purpose, Who works out everything in agreement with the counsel and design of His [own] will, So that we who first hoped in Christ [who first put our confidence in Him have been destined and appointed to] live for the praise of His glory!"

Ephesians 2:10 AMP:

"For we are God's [own] handiwork (His workmanship), recreated in Christ Jesus, [born anew] that we may do those good works which God predestined (planned beforehand) for us [taking paths which He prepared ahead of time], that we should walk in them [living the good life which He prearranged and made ready for us to live]."

Hebrews 3:14:

"For we have become fellows with Christ (the Messiah) and share in all He has for us, if only we hold our first newborn confidence and original assured expectation [in virtue of which we are believers] firm and unshaken to the end."

God has an obligation to Himself within His own heart that those He foreknew; those that He has predestinated, those that He ordained according to the ELECTION OF GRACE (Romans 5:11); He must conform to the image of His Son that they must show forth the praises of Him who called them out of darkness or obscurity into His LIGHT, HIS LIFE, and HIS LOVE.

Romans 8:29 AMP:

"For those whom He foreknew [of whom He was aware and loved beforehand], He also destined from the beginning [foreordaining them] to be molded into the image of His Son [and share inwardly His likeness], that He might become the firstborn among many brethren."

1 Peter 2:9 AMP:

"But you are a chosen race, a royal priesthood, a dedicated nation, [God's] own purchased, special people, that you may set forth the wonderful deeds and display the virtues and perfections of Him Who called you out of darkness into His marvelous light."

It is God's responsibility to finish what He has started in those that He has chosen. We did not chose Him first; He chose us first.

John 15:16 AMP:

"You have not chosen Me, but I have chosen you and I have appointed you [I have planted you], that you might go and bear fruit and keep on bearing, and that your fruit may be lasting [that it may remain, abide], so that whatever you ask the Father in My Name [as presenting all that I AM], He may give it to you."

2 Timothy 1:9 AMP:

"[For it is He] Who delivered and saved us and called us with a calling in itself holy and leading to holiness [to a life of consecration, a vocation of holiness]; [He did it] not because of anything of merit that we have done, but because of and to further His own purpose and grace (unmerited favor)

which was given us in Christ Jesus before the world began [eternal ages ago]. [It is that purpose and grace] which He now has made known and has fully disclosed and made real [to us] through the appearing of our Savior Christ Jesus, Who annulled death and made it of no effect and brought life and immortality (immunity from eternal death) to light through the Gospel. For [the proclaiming of] this [Gospel] I was appointed a herald (preacher) and an apostle (special messenger) and a teacher of the Gentiles." "Many are called, but few are chosen," (Matthew 22:14).

There is a process, a journey for those that have been chosen by God before the foundations of the world that is not for those that were not chosen. An example in the Old Testament is the twelve tribes known as the children of God, but only one tribe (Levi) was ordained by God as the priesthood, and only one linage of that tribe was chosen by God to qualify for the responsibility and position of going into the Holy of Holies.

> **Whom God has given much wisdom and responsibility to, He requires much from.**

The reason that God chooses is not to say that some have more special privilege than others or that they are more special to God, but that what God has given much wisdom/responsibility to, He requires much from.

Many of us are going through things that we cannot understand because we don't fit into the conformities of what the church requires. God not only created you in His image, but designed you to incorporate every detail in order to be transformed with His perfection that only He would be glorified while you were in your natural body on His earth.

God does not need to be fair. He is sovereign; He is ALL in ALL. God can bring ALL into His image as ALL. We can choose whether we want our eggs scrambled, boiled, or sunny-side up, but we will still be eating eggs. We can choose the journey or the limitations of what God has permitted, but the finished work is GOD ALL in ALL. We cannot even choose not to choose, but must choose within the realm of God's permitted choice for each of us.

You did not have any say in when you were born, who you would be when you were born (male or female), what time period or culture you would be born into, who your parents would be, your skin color, hair, height, or eye color. The church has taught us to think we can choose whether or not to carry His DNA within us (Luke 3:38). We might be able to change our hair color, but we cannot choose to change our DNA any more than we can change our blood type. (Ironically, even in changing our hair color, the real color will keep coming out at the roots.)

Did God ask you if you wanted to be chosen before the foundation of the world? Did He ask you if you wanted to be sent to the earth so that He could work hell out of you and put you in situations causing doubt and insecurity, wondering if you would make it back to heaven? Would we not have said, No thank you God? I choose to stay right where I'm at in spirit with the guarantee of being in heaven instead of the anxiety of wondering if I made the right choice in the flesh of making my way back. Let me just keep playing in heaven and hanging out with the heavenly host singing angelic songs. And whatever you do Father, keep me away from those double minded religious people that call themselves the church that bring death into heaven with their logic and reason.

Why would we want to "choose" to come out of eternity into time only to spend our LIFE in CHRIST with the devil? And then on top of all this "choice," according to the church, you might even spend your Christ Life eternally with satan. NO THANK YOU GOD, just let me stay in heaven as you foreknew me and created me before the foundations of the world (Ephesians 1:4).

If we truly have total choice, would we not choose things to bless us? If LIGHT, LIFE, and LOVE really are the fullness of what we search for, and if we already had them before we were conceived in our mother's womb, why would we choose to leave heaven?

Jeremiah 1:5 AMP:

"Before I formed you in the womb I knew [and] approved of you [as My chosen instrument], and before you were born I separated and set you apart, consecrating you; [and] I appointed you as a prophet to the nations)."

If God had shown us in advance while we were still in spirit, before the foundation of the world what our life would be like choosing to be born in time, we would have said, NO THANK YOU! But we didn't get that choice, God chose us. We must stop playing church, saying that we have a "choice," and start aligning ourselves with filling the earth with His glory as sons of God through Christ Jesus, ruling and reigning with HIM in heavenly places.

God created ALL the elements of matter. Each element has the basic parts of protons, neutrons, and electrons. However, God did not create all of them the same element. Yet, each element has a unique/divine place and position in the periodic table. The elements that He used to create the fish and the plants have many of the same chemical form that He used to create man, but the way they function together has produced a permanent creation of "kind" making it impossible for a cat to become a tree, or a dog to become a man. God created man in His image and likeness.

Genesis 1:25-27 AMP:

"And God made the [wild] beasts of the earth according to their kinds, and domestic animals according to their kinds, and everything that creeps upon the earth according to its kind. And God saw that it was good (fitting, pleasant) and He approved it. God said, Let Us [Father, Son, and Holy Spirit] make mankind in Our image, after Our likeness, and let them have complete authority over the fish of the sea, the birds of the air, the [tame] beasts, and over all of the earth, and over everything that creeps upon the earth. So God created man in His own image, in the image and likeness of God He created him; male and female He created them."

God answers our prayers according to His will and according to His purpose. What He has already accomplished He does not need to do again. Jesus Christ died once and for all, taking the government of sin and death upon Him to do away with it. Now, it is up to us to align ourselves with who He is, WORD, while in our natural body. It is time for transforming our soul and body into HIM (Christ in us/word) instead of warring against our own thoughts and imagination. If we were to try to jump out of a plane, and fly like an eagle without a parachute, we would die. Then if we were to ask God why He didn't save us from death, He would answer that He already did through Christ Jesus as a son of God, not as a bird or eagle, and that you created your own death acting as a "strange" Christian.

1 Corinthians 15:51-57 (The Message):

"But let me tell you something wonderful, a mystery I'll probably never fully understand. We're not all going to die-but we are all going to be changed. You hear a blast to end all blasts from a trumpet, and in the time that you look up and blink your eyes-it's over. On signal from that trumpet from heaven, the dead will be up and out of their graves, beyond the reach of death, never to die again. At the same moment and in the same way, we'll all be changed. In the resurrection scheme of things, this has to happen: everything perishable taken off the shelves and replaced by the imperishable, this mortal replaced by the immortal. Then the saying will come true: Death swallowed by triumphant Life! Who got the last word, oh, Death? Oh, Death, who's afraid of you now? It was sin that made death so frightening and law-code guilt that gave sin its leverage, its destructive power. But now in a single victorious stroke of Life, all three-sin, guilt, death-are gone, the gift of our Master, Jesus Christ. Thank God!"

Do you see where "death" began? As a "word" or thought that became flesh and was fed "in-form- ation" from the Tree of Knowledge of Good and Evil which allowed God's image (word/form) of LIFE the "form" of death.

In – within

Form - manifest, take on a definite shape/character/personality/identity

a-tion - individual who responds with the soul/emotions that reflects into their body (form).

The soul/emotions respond to our thoughts. Without thought, there is no "feeling." The cells of the body react to the thought that creates the emotion.

This is why Paul says in 1 Corinthians 2: 7-16:

"But we speak the wisdom of God in a mystery, even the hidden wisdom, which God ordained before the world unto our glory: Which none of the princes of this world knew: for had they known it, they would not have crucified the Lord of glory. But as it is written, Eye hath not seen, nor ear heard, neither have entered into the heart of man, the things which God hath prepared for them that love him. But God hath revealed them unto us by his Spirit: for the Spirit searches all things, yea, the deep things of God. For what man knoweth the things of a man, save the spirit of man which is in him? Even so the things of God knoweth no man, but the Spirit of God. Now we have received, not the spirit of the world, but the spirit which is of God; that we might know the things that are freely given to us of God.

Which things also we speak, not in the words which man's wisdom teacheth, but which the Holy Ghost teacheth; comparing spiritual things with spiritual. But the natural man receiveth not the things of the Spirit of God: for they are foolishness unto him: neither can he know them, because they are spiritually discerned. But he that is spiritual judgeth all things, yet he himself is judged of no man. For who hath known the mind of the Lord, that he may instruct him? But we have the mind of Christ."

Luke 9:57-59 AMP:

"And it occurred that as they were going along the road, a man said to Him, Lord, I will follow you wherever you go. And Jesus told him, Foxes have lurking holes and the birds of the air have roosts and nests, but the Son of

Man have no place to lay His head. And He said to another, Become My disciple, side with my party, and accompanies me! But he replied, Lord, permit me first to go and bury (await the death of) my father (my natural identity/death to my carnal body)."

Luke 9: 60-62 AMP:

"But Jesus said to him, allow the dead (those that are spiritually in the outer or middle court) *to bury their own* (your thoughts determine you) *dead; but as for you, go and publish abroad throughout all regions the kingdom of God. Another also said, I will follow You, Lord, and become your disciple and side with your party; but let me first say good-bye to those at my home. Jesus said to him, No one who puts his hand to the plow and looks back [to the things behind] is fit for the kingdom of God* (Entering into the throne room of God/the Holy of Holies). "

History reveals that God has always had a selected few that He has placed in certain times throughout the ages and caused them to walk a course of life that is different than the norm of their era. Many are called, but few are chosen (Matt. 22:14), and those that are chosen will have a sense of destiny, a divine calling, that drives them to see it fulfilled that others will not understand, and possibly consider them very strange, even questioning if they are of a cult.

The warfare these people battle within themselves is because they were chosen. This battle is the identity of Heaven brought into time, the Kingdom of God being manifested in this world. Their greatest enemy is not the non-believers, but those that "think" they are "good Christians" and feel threatened within their identity because they do not comprehend the same understanding of those that have been chosen. It is many times a challenge of the soul because those that are closest to a "chosen one" are creating the greatest battle out of jealousy and envy. Being "chosen" IS NOT a position of being greater than others or being more special to God than others. It is a position of humbleness and perseverance that requires denying one's self for the greater cause of bringing forth the sons of God in others.

There must be a beginning, and the beginning must be like God. The birth of the "sons of God" must come through a pregnancy that climaxes with travail. *"A woman when she is in travail hath sorrow, because her hour is come: but as soon as she is delivered of the child, she remembered no more the anguish, for joy that a man is born into the world"* (John 16:21). Paul tells us, *"My little children, of whom I travail in birth again until Christ be formed in you"* (Galatians 4:19).

If the beginning is God and the end is God, He is all in ALL (1 Corinthians 15:28). There must be an identity of God manifested in every age to bring unity of the ALL. *"There are diversities of operations, but it is the same God which worked all in all"* (1 Corinthians 12:6). Therefore, if the beginning is God, then it is finished before it is started. If God is going to create the perfect offspring, He has already created the perfect seed. For God to be righteous, just, and truly sovereign having His way at the end, the beginning must be ALL God so that the end has no other conclusion.

Since God begins with sovereignty and operates in ways that are foolish to our carnal understanding, we must accept by faith that within His sovereignty contains the perfect seed of God that is His Divine plan. Since the finished work of God has to be God, the end must be the fullness of the beginning, which is God. Within His sovereignty is the journey of the perfect seed being manifested in a process that concludes that *"Christ is all, and in all"* (Colossians 3:11)

"For it is God which worked in you both to will and to do of his good pleasure" (Phil. 2:13). When we say "yes" to God, it is only because He has already said "yes" to us. *"And the LORD stirred up the spirit of Zerubbabel the son of Shealtiel, governor of Judah, and the spirit of Joshua the son of Josedech, the high priest, and the spirit of all the remnant of the people; and they came and did work in the house of the LORD of hosts, their God"* (Haggai 1:14).

Those whom God has chosen will not fit in the normal environment of the church world. They will be frustrated and restless sitting in church services that are on time limitations and rituals. They will constantly be seeking an in-depth relationship with God that goes so far beyond what others desire that many times they will find their journey independently in order to bring into the corporate body a greater awakening *"to whom God would make known what is the riches of the glory of this mystery among the Gentiles; which is Christ in you, the hope of glory"* (Colossians 1:27).

God calls this predestined. "The election of grace." *"Even so then at this present time also there is a remnant according to the election of grace"* (Romans 11:5). We learn that those things that we are going through do include choice and consequences, but there is also a persistent predetermined destiny that draws us with a desire that goes beyond who we are, and for the sake of Christ, we make righteous choices that transform the body of Christ into His image.

This transformation of the body of Christ must become experiential. This is not something we read in a book and claim it as ours, a word of faith we accept, or a sinner's prayer where we receive Jesus into our heart. It is through the trials and tribulations that we are able to put aside our carnal way and seek "the joy of the Lord as our strength." Out of our inner most realm, our thoughts are transformed into His peace that surpasses ALL of our understanding, and LIFE is birthed.

This is working out of the Spirit of God within us according to His good pleasure. *"He who believes in Me [who cleaves to and trusts in and relies on Me] as the Scripture has said, from his innermost being shall flow [continuously] springs and rivers of living water"* (John 7:38 AMP).

Taking another look at 1 Peter 5:10-11 (AMP*): "And after you have suffered a little while, the God of all grace [Who imparts all blessing and favor], Who has called you to His [own] eternal glory in Christ Jesus, will Himself complete and make you what you ought to be, establish and ground you securely, and strengthen, and settle you. To Him be the dominion (power, authority, rule) forever and ever. Amen (so be it)."*

Suf - sub or under

Fer - to bare

Suffer = to bare under, to be subjected to a certain trial. However, despite the trial or suffering, God's election of grace is equal to bring us through that trial and greater to raise us up and beyond the trial allowing us to KNOW the POWER of HIS RESURRECTED LIFE IN OUR LIVES.

Philippians 3:9-11 (AMP):

"And that I may [actually] be found and known as in Him, not having any [self-achieved] righteousness that can be called my own, based on my obedience to the Law's demands (ritualistic uprightness and supposed right standing with God thus acquired), but possessing that [genuine righteousness] which comes through faith in Christ (the Anointed One), the [truly] right standing with God, which comes from God by [saving] faith.[For my determined purpose is] that I may know Him [that I may progressively become more deeply and intimately acquainted with Him, perceiving and recognizing and understanding the wonders of His Person more strongly and more clearly], and that I may in that same way come to know the power out flowing from His resurrection [which it exerts over believers], and that I may so share His sufferings as to be continually transformed [in spirit into His likeness even] to His death, [in the hope].That if possible I may attain to the [spiritual and moral] resurrection [that lifts me] out from among the dead [even while in the body]."

The election of grace tells us that regardless of what we go through, His grace is sufficient. Many Christians claim Romans 8:14-17a which says:

"For as many as are led by the Spirit of God, they are the sons of God. For ye have not received the spirit of bondage again to fear; but ye have received the Spirit of adoption, whereby we cry, Abba, Father. The Spirit itself beareth witness with our spirit, that we are the children of God: And if children, then heirs; heirs of God, and joint-heirs with Christ."

However, as much as we desire to be known as a "King's kid," very few want to go through the rest of what Paul wrote to truly obtain the inheritance that is ours.

Romans 8: 17b-30:

"If so be that we suffer with him, that we may be also glorified together. For I reckon that the sufferings of this present time are not worthy to be compared with the glory which shall be revealed in us. For the earnest expectation of the creature waiteth for the manifestation of the sons of God. For the creature was made subject to vanity, not willingly, but by reason of him who hath subjected the same in hope, Because the creature itself also shall be delivered from the bondage of corruption into the glorious liberty of the children of God. For we know that the whole creation groaneth and travailed in pain together until now. And not only they, but ourselves also, which have the firstfruits of the Spirit, even we ourselves groan within ourselves, waiting for the adoption, to wit, the redemption of our body. For we are saved by hope: but hope that is seen is not hope: for what a man seeth, why doth he yet hope for? But if we hope for that we see not, then do we with patience wait for it. Likewise the Spirit also helpeth our infirmities: for we know not what we should pray for as we ought: but the Spirit itself maketh intercession for us with groaning which cannot be uttered.

And he that searches the hearts knoweth what is the mind of the Spirit, because he maketh intercession for the saints according to the will of God. And we know that all things work together for good to them that love God, to them who are the called according to his purpose. For whom he did foreknow, he also did predestinate to be conformed to the image of his Son, that he might be the firstborn among many brethren. Moreover whom he did predestinate, them he also called: and whom he called, them he also justified: and whom he justified, them he also glorified."

Take note that as we suffer with Him, the glorification He received, we receive also. However, this is not a "someday when we get to heaven" glorification. If we re-read what Paul wrote in Romans 8:18 AMP, *"[But what of that?] For I consider that the sufferings of this present time (this present life) are not worth being compared with the glory that is about to be revealed to us and in us and for us and conferred on us,"* that the glory of God is revealed "to us, in us, for us, and on us" NOW.

We may each be unique individuals, but we all have only one Father. It is He who is working according to His good pleasure in you (Philippians 2:13), having predestinated us unto the adoption of children by Jesus Christ to Himself (Ephesians 1:5), and having made known in us the mystery of His will, according to His good pleasure which He already purposed in Himself (Ephesians 1:9). No other power can bring into fulfillment what God predestined in you before the foundation of the world. It is His love that will draw us to His predestined finished work that was completed before it began as Christ is ALL in ALL.

Psalms 91:14, *"Because he hath set his love upon me, therefore will I deliver him: I will set him on high, because he hath known my name."*

Isaiah 63:9, *"In all their affliction he was afflicted, and the angel of his presence saved them: in his love and in his pity he redeemed them; and he bare them, and carried them all the days of old."*

Zephaniah 3:17, *"The LORD thy God in the midst of thee is mighty; he will save, he will rejoice over thee with joy; he will rest in his love, he will joy over thee with singing."*

Romans 5:8, *"But God commanded his love toward us, in that, while we were yet sinners, Christ died for us."*

Galatians 6:14, *"But far be it from me to glory [in anything or anyone] except in the cross of our Lord Jesus Christ (the Messiah) through whom the world has been crucified to me, and I to the world!"*

Philippians 1:11, *"May you abound in and be filled with the fruits of righteousness (of right standing with God and right doing) which come through Jesus Christ (the Anointed One), to the honor and praise of God [that His glory may be both manifested and recognized]."*

Hebrews 1:9, *"You have loved righteousness [You have delighted in integrity, virtue, and uprightness in purpose, thought, and action] and you have hated lawlessness (injustice and iniquity). Therefore God, [even] Your God (Godhead), has anointed you with the oil of exultant joy and gladness above and beyond your companions."*

Selah

Chapter 16

The Vision of a New Beginning:

A personal vision from the Holy Spirit

---

*"In the last days, God says, I will pour out my Spirit on all people.
Your sons and daughters will prophesy, your young men will
see visions, your old men will dream dreams."*

Acts 2:17

The vision begins with me looking at a clay flowerpot floating in the air. The pot was gently moving as it was carried by the wind on a clear day— no rain or clouds, just wind. I find myself along the side of the pot and together the wind takes us on a soothing journey with no cares or concerns. This gave me an opportunity to focus and take a closer look at the pot. I saw on the outside of this clay vessel a very strong, silver-linked chain wrapped around it. It looked like the chain was holding the pot together because I could also see hairline cracks in the clay. When I looked closer to each link, I noticed the Greek symbols for Alpha and Omega made their formation.

Next, my eyes went from looking at the side of the pot to focusing upward to the lip portion of the vessel. I noticed there were words written in a language that I was able to understand with a Greek font. The words "LIFE AND DEATH LIFE AND DEATH LIFE AND DEATH" were carved into the clay as it circled the entire rim. The wind began to take me a little higher than the pot, which allowed me to look inside. I was surprised not to see any dirt or a plant. Instead, I found smooth black stones piled on top of each other. They were dry and dusty as if they had been baking in the sun.

As I looked closely at the stones, I noticed a glow was coming out from their midst. At first I did not see anything but black stones, but then this glow became a small LIGHT rising and getting brighter, like a plant emerging from the soil. As the LIGHT emerged, it was surrounded by a plate of glass that separated it from the black stones. As the LIGHT got brighter and brighter, a distinct aroma began to fill my nostrils with the scent of fresh cut roses. I closed my eyes to enjoy this fragrance. This posture of rest gave me peace and comfort. When I opened my eyes, I was no longer above the clay pot, but within the midst of it *with* the LIGHT.

There was an awe of silence and peace all around me that I cannot describe by my natural thoughts. I looked at my hands and feet and noticed my body had on the same clothes I was familiar with while outside this clay vessel, but now they looked different, with a freshness and cleanliness that no amount of washing could have done. Again, something I could not explain, but simply accepted with the presence of where I was at.

I turned away from the center of the LIGHT to view my surroundings, and found myself able to look through the glass. I noticed that the black stones no longer looked black as they did when I was outside the clay pot, but where stones of an array of many colors (blue, purple, orange, green, yellow, and red). These colors where not solid, but had a transparency glow that changed the boundaries of the formation of the stones. I noticed that as I moved closer to the glass, the color of the stones would change to white. I also noticed that the glass simply vanished to where I could actually extend my hand and touch the stones. As soon as my fingers made contact with the stones, their boundaries of form diminished allowing my hand to penetrate within them. A succession of LIGHT began traveling, going beyond the stone that I touched to the stones around it. All the black stones took on a transformation of arrays of glowing color that became so intense that all that was visible was the transfiguration into LIGHT.

Suddenly, a noise filled the atmosphere that broke the silence. It was not a fearful noise, but one that transforms death into LIFE. The chain links around the clay vessel broke and the pot itself shattered. The stones were released into the air in their metamorphous form. They filled the earth as LIGHT replacing darkness.

The Holy Spirit showed me that these black stones were diamonds in the rough. When the presence of God comes into the presence of man, every knee will bow and every tongue will confess that Jesus Christ is Lord, filling the earth with the glory (sons) of God.

I heard the voice of God say, "I am not interested in making something right, for then there must be something wrong, but manifesting wholeness which comes by faith in believing I AM. Everything I AM is ETERNAL, not a one-time event. Within each of My creations is My "Holy Thing" that was also in Mary. Jesus Christ is My only begotten Son in whom I AM well pleased. I have resurrected my WORD where death has no power. The fullness of MY body is being transformed with the presence of ME, and the death of emptiness has been filled with "Let My Will Be Done According to Your Word." Out of the heart My mouth will speak filling the atmosphere with My heart, My identity, My nature, where every knee will bow and every tongue will confess that Jesus Christ is Lord of ALL. I AM removing the veil of blindness (race, religion, politics, economics, and gender) and opening the eyes of MY LOVE and MERCY from the inner most part of my throne to give power and authority to those that call me ABBA. I move by faith, not by sight. Faith is the evidence of THINGS hoped for. How big is your faith? What is the hope of your desire and calling? Nothing is impossible to me for those that believe.

Selah

Chapter 17

Manifesting His Name

"Which were born, not of blood, nor of the will of the flesh, nor of the will of man, but of God. And the Word was made flesh, and dwelt among us, (and we beheld his glory, the glory as of the only begotten of the Father,) full of grace and truth."

John 1:13-14

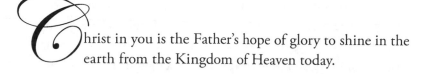

hrist in you is the Father's hope of glory to shine in the earth from the Kingdom of Heaven today.

"For unto us (you and me) a child is born, unto us (you and me) a son is given: and the government shall be upon his shoulder: and his name shall be called Wonderful, Counselor, The mighty God, The everlasting Father, and the Prince of Peace" (Isaiah 9:6).

"But thou (you), Bethlehem Ephratah (fruitfulness), though thou (you) be little(inferior) among the thousands of Judah, yet out of thee (you and me) shall he(Christ) come forth unto me (Almighty God) that is to be ruler in Israel; whose goings forth have been from of old, from everlasting. Therefore will he give them up, until the time (season) that she (the bride/wife of Christ) which travailed hath brought forth: then the remnant of his brethren shall return unto the children (sons) of Israel. And he shall stand and feed (shepherds) in the strength of the LORD (Jehovah), in the majesty of the name of the LORD (Jehovah) his God (Elohim); and they shall abide (dwell): for now shall he be great unto the ends (limits) of the earth (land), and this man shall be (comes to be) the peace" (Micah 5:2-5).

As we read and study these scriptures written by the prophets, Isaiah and Micah, we can find some hidden understanding of what was foretold before Jesus was born. For centuries we have read the prophetic word in Isaiah 9:6 with an acceptance of our Christian heritage to celebrate Christmas.

Unfortunately, we use the celebration as an excuse to take time off from work and to spend money, justifying the season by going to a Christmas Eve service. Then, once the holiday is over, we are left with the debt to pay off for spending beyond our means for the sake of saying, "But it's Christmas, and it comes only once a year."

Is this what God desired for us when this prophecy was given?

Many people have gone to another extreme to say that Christians are celebrating a pagan holiday and that December 25th wasn't really the birth of Jesus, but an excuse to justify a means of when he was born. Interestingly, these same people are huge on celebrating the Passover season—the death of Jesus on the cross. So when did He enter the world to be put Him on the cross if we don't have a Christmas birth?

This prophecy says to "us," that's you and me, a child was born, and this child is a son that has the unique name of God: I AM.

Then when we read these scriptures in Micah, we can understand more specifically that the birth of this son whose name is the unique name of God, I AM, will be born from a woman who is in travail. Well, if we only give this scripture a reference to Mary, the mother of Jesus of Nazareth, then we can close these prophecies and consider the scriptures are fulfilled and we don't need to consider them anymore.

Hmm...Is not God Spirit? Is not God Eternal, Everlasting? Is not the Word of God the Life of God? Then how can we limit what God is doing today by justifying that these scriptures only pertain to a child born possibly on December 25th in a manger from a woman named Mary?

History has shown us that the Gospels of Matthew, Mark, and Luke were written within a very close time period around 60A.D. before the fall of Jerusalem. The Gospel of John comes along approximately 20-25 years later, written around the same time that the Book of Revelation and the Letters of John are written.

An interesting assessment of these four Gospels is that Mark was written first, and then Matthew uses Mark's writing and plugs in his version and understanding. About the same time, Luke is doing the same thing. This is why we can read the same events in these three Gospels, but each one has some variation. Then we have John's Gospel almost a generation later and after the destruction of Jerusalem.

What we will find is, like before, John did not change anything that the other three had written, but he plugged in some key information that, without it, we would miss the links of what the birth, death, and resurrection of Jesus Christ was all about. For example, without these following key scriptures with which John starts his writing, we wouldn't know that the purpose of the cross and resurrection of Jesus Christ was to bring man back to Genesis chapters one and two.

"In the beginning was the Word, and the Word was with God, and the Word was God. The same was in the beginning with God. All things were made by him; and without him was not anything made that was made" (John 1:1-3)

"Which were born, not of blood, nor of the will of the flesh, nor of the will of man, but of God. And the Word was made flesh, and dwelt among us, (and we beheld his glory, the glory as of the only begotten of the Father,) full of grace and truth" (John 1:13-14).

John lets us know that Jesus of Nazareth was born from a woman named Mary, but the WORD made flesh that dwells among men was not born of blood like humanities way of creating life.

Remember, we just read in Micah that He comes in the majesty of the name of God. Something to remember is that a name carries nature, identity, and attributes. When we hear the name Jehovah it means "He who IS...becomes." God told Moses in Exodus 3:14a-15b, *"I AM WHO I AM: This is my name, and this is my memorial unto all generations."* Another way of saying this is, "I BECOME WHOM I BECOME."

By this name, God identifies His plan for all generations. Micah prophesies that in the majesty of the name of Jehovah is His Elohim. The name of God, Elohim, is describing the creative, purpose, and plurality attribute of Jehovah. The supreme, Almighty Lord God manifests, and once He manifests, He is our Elohim. The name Elohim stands in the strength of He who has become HIM.

"In the beginning God (Elohim) created the heaven and the earth" (Genesis 1:1).

"In the beginning was the Word (Logos), and the Word was with God (Elohim), and the Word was God (Elohim). The same was in the beginning with God (Elohim). All things were made by Him (Elohim); and without him (Elohim) was not anything made that was made. In him (Elohim) was life; and the life (Elohim life) was the light of men" (John 1:1-4).

Here is where the hardship of our lives begins. It begins with having the experience of oneness with Christ. There are many who know about Jesus Christ crucified, buried, and resurrected from the dead, but very few have experienced the intimacy of knowing that Paul describes in Galatians 2:20 AMP, *"I have been crucified with Christ [in Him I have shared His crucifixion]; it is no longer I who live, but Christ (the Messiah) lives in me; and the life I now live in the body I live by faith in (by adherence to and reliance on and complete trust in) the Son of God, Who loved me and gave Himself up for me."*

Paul also shares in Philippians 3:9-11AMP:

"That I may [actually] be found and known as in Him, not having any [self-achieved] righteousness that can be called my own, based on my obedience to the Law's demands (ritualistic uprightness and supposed right standing with God thus acquired), but possessing that [genuine righteousness] which comes through faith in Christ (the Anointed One), the [truly] right standing with God, which comes from God by [saving] faith. [For my determined purpose is] that I may know Him [that I may progressively become more deeply and intimately acquainted with Him, perceiving and recognizing and understanding the wonders of His Person more strongly and more clearly], and that I may in that same way come to know the power outflowing from His resurrection [which it exerts over believers], and that I may so share His sufferings as to be continually transformed [in spirit into His likeness even] to His death, [in the hope]. That if possible I may attain to the [spiritual and moral] resurrection [that lifts me] out from among the dead [even while in the body]."

The "knowing" that Paul refers to is not intellectual knowledge, but has the same meaning of the Hebrew word used in Genesis 4:1 when Adam "knew" Eve, and she conceived a son.

The amazing gift we have been given is **Christ in us;** the hope of glory bringing unity of Christ with the Father. This is the awesomeness of God's amazing grace that has nothing to do with our goodness, but the greatness of God's love for us.

Jesus stands in the strength of which He has become, Elohim, in whom He has become one with us: Christ in you is the glory to be manifested that as He is, so are you in this world today (1 John 4:17). Jesus of Nazareth knew this intimacy though he had natural family on the earth. Often, those who are close to us are the ones that have the most difficulty accepting this truth because they know our history. Jesus stood in the strength of Jehovah,

the majestic name of Elohim, with whom He has become as one, which gave Him the ability to say, *"When you have seen me, you have seen the Father"* (John 14:9).

We have thousands of sermons, books, and teachings that have been shared throughout history about Jesus Christ, but how many have really "known" HIM? There are many male doctors in the world that can tell you how to have a baby, but how many of them have had the experience? Today we have the inheritance to know and experience the power of the resurrection of Jesus Christ while in our natural body, but very few of us want to give birth to it, letting go of our self-ego allowing the oneness of the body of Christ to come together in the unity of His faith, Life, and Love that He gave to us over 2,000 years ago at Calvary.

In Psalm 22, King David wrote a prophecy about the crucifixion of Jesus Christ. In verse 22 of this Psalm we read, *"I will declare (speak of the facts) Your name to my brethren; in the midst of the congregation will I praise You."*

In Isaiah 30: 27-31 we read:

"Behold, the Name of the Lord comes from afar, burning with His anger, and in thick, rising smoke. His lips are full of indignation, and His tongue is like a consuming fire. And His breath is like an overflowing stream that

reaches even to the neck, to sift the nations with the sieve of destruction; and a bridle that causes them to err will be in the jaws of the people. You shall have a song as in the night when a holy feast is kept, and gladness of heart as when one marches in procession with a flute to go to the temple on the mountain of the Lord, to the Rock of Israel. And the Lord shall cause His glorious voice to be heard and the descending blow of His arm to be seen, coming down with indignant anger and with the flame of a devouring fire, amid crashing blast and cloudburst, tempest, and hailstones. At the voice of the Lord the Assyrians will be stricken with dismay and terror, when He smites them with His rod."

What is interesting about these scriptures is that many people only "know" God as vengeance and wrath, but the reality is a name comes forth when consummation (knowing experience) occurs. Jehovah God makes Himself known in righteous manifestation (Psalm 96:13).

"I will strengthen them (give them mastery) in the LORD (Jehovah their Elohim); and they shall walk up and down in his name (Elohim), says the LORD (Jehovah)" (Zechariah 10:12).

The name declares the identity, the authority, and the position of the person. In them, He has become, and in them He will walk in this world (1 John 4:17). They become the plurality of Elohim walking in His person, His nature, and His authority.

Many believers in Christ use the name of Jesus in prayer, but they do not walk AS HE IS, in the intimate knowledge of HIM, AS ONE in the world. Yet there is a company of believers that have separated themselves from the complacency of the church and are rising up with the "knowing" oneness that Christ is in them and has become them in this world.

"For all people will walk everyone in the name of his god (there will always be those that have other gods), and (however) we (there are those that God has separated from the world) will walk in the name of the LORD our God for ever and ever" (Micah 4:5).

"Blessed is he (you and me), whosoever shall not be offended places boundaries) in me (the name of Jesus Christ)" (Luke 7:23).

"I declare to you, you will not see Me (Jesus Christ) again until you say, Blessed (magnified in worship, adored, and exalted) is He (Christ in you) Who comes in the name of the Lord!" (Matthew 23:39 AMP).

The very same love that the Father has for Jesus Christ, Christ Jesus has for you. You are His body, bone of His bone, and flesh of His flesh.

"In many separate revelations [each of which set forth a portion of the Truth] and in different ways God spoke of old to [our] forefathers in and by the prophets, [But] in the last of these days He has spoken to us in [the person of a] Son, whom He appointed Heir and lawful Owner of all things, also by and through Whom He created the worlds and the reaches of space and the ages of time [He made, produced, built, operated, and arranged them in order]. He is the sole expression of the glory of God [the Light-being, the out-raying or radiance of the divine], and He is the perfect imprint and very image of [God's] nature, upholding and maintaining and guiding and propelling the universe by His mighty word of power" (Hebrews 1:1-3AMP).The fullness of why Jesus Christ came into this world as a baby in the flesh, died on the cross, was buried, and then rose from the dead can be explained by the prophecy of Psalm 22:22 where we read again, *"I will declare Your name to my brethren; in the midst of the congregation will I praise You."*

The fulfillment of this was spoken by Jesus in John 17. Again, keep in mind that when Matthew, Mark, Luke and Paul's Epistles were written and passed around to share the Gospel of Jesus Christ, John's Gospel had not yet been included as we have it today. This prayer of Jesus to the Father was not unveiled to man until after Jerusalem fell, approximately 20 years after the other Gospels and Paul's letters had been in circulation.

"O righteous Father, the world hath not known thee: but I have known thee, and these have known that thou hast sent me. And I have declared unto

them thy name, and will declare it: that the love wherewith thou hast loved me may be in them, and I in them" (John 17:25-26).

Notice that Jesus Christ has finished the declaration of the Father's name prophesied in Psalm 22:22, and He continues to declare that the love of God would be in them (you and me), and that I (Elohim) would be in you and me. The very same love that God has for Jesus Christ has for us, and Christ is in us.

Jesus says in John 17:6-8:

"I have manifested thy name (Elohim, the name and nature of the Father) unto the people (you and me) which thou gave them me out of the world: Yours they were, and You gave them me (John 3:16); and they have kept thy word (logos). Now they have known that all things whatsoever thou hast given me are of thee. For I have given unto them the words which thou gave me; and they have received them, and have known surely that I came out from thee, and they have believed that thou didst send me."

This is not just about a baby being born, or Emmanuel, *"God with us,"* but it is saying "God gave you and me Elohim, and we have kept Him. He who is, becomes Jehovah— our Elohim. Jesus Christ our Lord, He who is Jehovah, becomes our Elohim— Christ in You."

John 8:58, *"Jesus said unto them, Verily, verily, I say unto you, Before Abraham was, I am."*

Exodus 6:7, *"I will take you to me as a people (I will become a people in you), and I will be to you as God (Elohim): and you will realize, know, and experience that I am Jehovah your Elohim, which brings you out from under the burdens of the Egyptians (bondages of this world)."*

Until we come to this revelation, heaven and earth will be separated in our hearts and we will seek a death of our body to be with God somewhere on the other side. However, when the prayer that we so often have said by memory becomes a reality to our spirit, *"Our Father who art in heaven, be your name. Let your kingdom come and let your will be come in earth as it already is in heaven,"* we open up the windows of heaven for the coming of the Lord.

God is Spirit. He is omnipresent. He is just as much in our midst today as He will be when "we die to go be with the Lord."

Unto you a child is born, and unto you a son is given. The church is the body of Christ Jesus, His bride and wife to carry the word. For each of us, in the fullness of time the rivers of living water will flow, circumcising the heart and out of our mouths we will declare, *"Blessed (magnified in worship, adored, and exalted) is He (Christ in you) Who comes in the name of the Lord!"*

"You Father have given ME power over all flesh, that I should give eternal life to as many as You have given ME. And this is life eternal, that they would know You the only true God, and Jesus Christ, whom You have sent. I have glorified You on the earth: I have finished (John 19:30) the work which You gave me to do. And now, O Father, glorify ME with Your own self with the glory which I had with You before the world was. I have manifested Your name (Elohim) in the people which You gave me out of the world: thine they were, and You gave them me (Elohim); and they have kept Your word (Your name, nature, and authority)" (John 17:2-6).

Jesus Christ has given us the power to become Life Eternal NOW.

In the beginning God (Elohim) was the WORD, and the WORD was made flesh.

"Holy Father, keep through Your own name those whom You hast given me, that they may be one, as we are" (John 17:11).

Selah

Chapter 18

The Bridegroom's Wedding:

The Wedding song of Christ

"Go ye therefore into the highways, and as many as ye shall find, bid to the marriage. So those servants went out into the highways, and gathered together all as many as they found, both bad and good: and the wedding was furnished with guests. And when the king came in to see the guests, he saw there a man which had not on a wedding garment: And he saith unto him, Friend, how come thou in hither not having a wedding garment? And he was speechless. Then said the king to the servants, Bind him hand and foot, and take him away, and cast him into outer darkness, there shall be weeping and gnashing of teeth. For many are called, but few are chosen." (Matthew 22:9-14).

Craftons – garments given to the guest at the door to be properly dressed for the King's wedding or banquet. No one has an excuse not to have the proper clothing for the wedding as the king would give it to the guest freely.

There is a connection with the garment that was worn and the character of the person wearing the garment.

Psalm 45 (Message)

A Wedding Song of the Sons of Korah (God has been making us a garment stitch by stitch in preparation for the marriage feast)

My heart bursts its banks, spilling beauty and goodness.
I pour it out in a poem to the king,
Shaping the river into words:

"You're the handsomest of men;
Every word from your lips is sheer grace,
And God has blessed you, blessed you so much.
Strap your sword to your side, warrior!
Accept praise! Accept due honor!
Ride majestically! Ride triumphantly!

Ride on the side of truth!
Ride for the righteous meek!

"Your instructions are glow-in-the-dark; you
shoot sharp arrows
Into enemy hearts; the king's
Foes lie down in the dust, beaten.

"Your throne is God's throne,
ever and always;
The scepter of your royal rule
measures right living.
You love the right
and hate the wrong.
And that is why God, your very own God,
poured fragrant oil on your head,
Marking you out as king
From among your dear companions.

"Your ozone-drenched garments are
fragrant with mountain breeze.
Chamber music—from the throne room—
makes you want to dance.
Kings' daughters are maids in your court,
the Bride glittering with golden jewelry.

"Now listen, daughter, don't miss a word: forget
your country, put your home behind you.
Be here—the king is wild for you.
Since he's your lord, adore him.
Wedding gifts pour in from Tyre;
Rich guests shower you with presents."

(Her wedding dress is dazzling, lined
with gold by the weavers;
All her dresses and robes are woven with gold.

She is led to the king,
Followed by her virgin companions. A procession of joy and
laughter!
A grand entrance to the king's palace!)

"Set your mind now on sons— don't
dote on father and grandfather.
You'll set your sons up as princes
all over the earth.
I'll make you famous for generations;
you'll be the talk of the town
For a long, long time."

In Luke 1 the words "espoused, betrothed" and engaged the promise of marriage. This promise requires wearing the "right" garment in preparation for the marriage feast.

Isaiah 61 proclaims a season of promise in preparation for the bride:

Isaiah 61 (KJV)

The Good News of Salvation

"The Spirit of the Lord GOD is upon Me,
because the LORD has anointed Me
To preach good tidings to the poor;
He has sent Me to heal the brokenhearted,
To proclaim liberty to the captives,
And the opening of the prison to those who are bound;
To proclaim the acceptable year of the LORD,
and the day of vengeance of our God;
To comfort all who mourn,
To console those who mourn in Zion, to
give them beauty for ashes,
The oil of joy for mourning,
The garment of praise for the spirit of heaviness;
that they may be called trees of righteousness,

The planting of the LORD, that He may be glorified."
And they shall rebuild the old ruins,
they shall raise up the former desolations,
and they shall repair the ruined cities, the
desolations of many generations.
Strangers shall stand and feed your flocks,
and the sons of the foreigner
Shall be your plowmen and your vinedressers.
But you shall be named the priests of the LORD,
They shall call you the servants of our God.
You shall eat the riches of the Gentiles,
and in their glory you shall boast.
Instead of your shame you shall have double honor,
And instead of confusion they shall rejoice in their portion.
Therefore in their land they shall possess double;
Everlasting joy shall be theirs.
"For I, the LORD, love justice;
I hate robbery for burnt offering; I will direct their work in truth,
And will make with them an everlasting covenant.
Their descendants shall be known among the Gentiles,
and their offspring among the people.
All who see them shall acknowledge them,
That they are the posterity whom the LORD has blessed."
I will greatly rejoice in the LORD, My
soul shall be joyful in my God;
For He has clothed me with the garments of salvation,
He has covered me with the robe of righteousness, as
a bridegroom decks himself with ornaments, And
as a bride adorns herself with her jewels.
For as the earth brings forth its bud,
As the garden causes the things that are sown in it to spring forth,
So the Lord GOD will cause righteousness and praise to spring forth
    before all the nations.

In the season of promise there is a celebration made in advance. When we celebrate the promise before it happens, we celebrate God. When we celebrate when it happens, it is the event being celebrated, not God.

What makes the celebration is the preparation before, being adorned stitch by stitch. Celebrating the journey to the day of the marriage is celebrating God in secret (counting it ALL joy in the midst of trials).

A bride is a bride for one day, then she is a wife. A woman is adorned with carrying the preparation of become a mother for nine months, then she is no longer a pregnant woman, but a mother.

When we begin to be a people that believe and speak things by faith that are not yet tangible, when we begin to praise God for things that are yet to appear, when we begin to go out on our journeys, taking our trumpets along because there is an expectance of a celebration as we are going towards the marriage (not during or after the marriage), then we celebrate God's fulfillment.

When the marriage finally occurs, and the celebration has come to a close, and responsibility takes place of consummating the marriage, the preparation becomes for a new generation.

The preparation of the marriage had nothing to do with the consummation. All the preparation for the marriage was about coming together and celebrating for what is yet to be. This is a time of celebrating and believing what is yet to take place. Once we as the bride of Christ consummate the marriage of the lamb, we are not brides anymore, but expectant mothers with a responsibility to raise the children. It is not about us, but HIM, raising the children to hear the voice of their Father.

People are waiting for something to happen to celebrate the coming of the Lord for the marriage supper of the Lamb, but because they are waiting instead of celebrating the preparation, we are missing the real celebration of transforming us into His image to be one with Him that must take place before the marriage is consummated.

Only God can go into the Holy of Holies. The celebrating incites this happening…the joy of the Lord is our strength in the midst of trials, working patience, patience produces experience, and experience produces hope. Hope produces faith, bringing forth the manifestation of God's love in us which produces LIFE.

God is looking for people to declare, behold the bridegroom comes.

Luke 4: 16-21:

So He came to Nazareth, where He had been brought up. And as His custom was, He went into the synagogue on the Sabbath day, and stood up to read. [17] *And He was handed the book of the prophet Isaiah. And when He had opened the book, He found the place where it was written:*

> *"The Spirit of the LORD is upon Me, Because He has anointed Me*
> *To preach the gospel to the poor;*
> *He has sent Me to heal the brokenhearted,*
> *proclaim liberty to the captives*
> *And recovery of sight to the blind,*
> *To set at liberty those who are oppressed;*
> *To proclaim the acceptable year of the LORD."*

20 Then He closed the book, and gave it back to the attendant and sat down. And the eyes of all who were in the synagogue were fixed on Him. 21 And He began to say to them, "Today this Scripture is fulfilled in your hearing."

Jesus closed the book because that portion of the prophecy was fulfilled. The rest of the prophecy is the marriage feast of the lamb-kin.

Continued in Isaiah 61:2b:

> *And the day of vengeance of our God;*
> *to comfort all who mourn,*
> *To console those who mourn in Zion,*
> *To give them beauty for ashes,*

the oil of joy for mourning,
The garment of praise for the spirit of heaviness;
that they may be called trees of righteousness,
The planting of the LORD, that He may be glorified."
And they shall rebuild the old ruins,
they shall raise up the former desolations,
and they shall repair the ruined cities, the
desolations of many generations.
Strangers shall stand and feed your flocks,
And the sons of the foreigner
Shall be your plowmen and your vinedressers.
6 But you shall be named the priests of the LORD,
They shall call you the servants of our God.
You shall eat the riches of the Gentiles,
and in their glory you shall boast.
Instead of your shame you shall have double honor,
And instead of confusion they shall rejoice in their portion.
Therefore in their land they shall possess double;
Everlasting joy shall be theirs.
"For I, the LORD, love justice;
I hate robbery for burnt offering;
I will direct their work in truth,
And will make with them an everlasting covenant.
Their descendants shall be known among the Gentiles,
and their offspring among the people.
All who see them shall acknowledge them,
That they are the posterity whom the LORD has blessed."
I will greatly rejoice in the LORD, My
soul shall be joyful in my God;
For He has clothed me with the garments of salvation,
He has covered me with the robe of righteousness,
As a bridegroom decks himself with ornaments,
And as a bride adorns herself with her jewels.
1 For as the earth brings forth its bud,
As the garden causes the things that are sown in it to spring forth,

So the Lord GOD will cause righteousness and praise to spring forth
before all the nations.

Isaiah 62

Assurance of Zion's Salvation

For Zion's sake I will not hold My peace,
And for Jerusalem's sake I will not rest,
Until her righteousness goes forth as brightness, and
her salvation as a lamp that burns.
The Gentiles shall see your righteousness,
And all kings your glory.
You shall be called by a new name,
Which the mouth of the LORD will name.
You shall also be a crown of glory
in the hand of the LORD,
And a royal diadem
In the hand of your God.
You shall no longer be termed Forsaken,
Nor shall your land any more be termed Desolate;
But you shall be called Hephzibah, and your land Beulah,
For the LORD delights in you,
And your land shall be married.
For as a young man marries a virgin,
so shall your sons marry you;
And as the bridegroom rejoices over the bride,
so shall your God rejoice over you.
I have set watchmen on your walls, O Jerusalem;
They shall never hold their peace day or night.
You who make mention of the LORD, do not keep silent,
And give Him no rest till He establishes
And till He makes Jerusalem a praise in the earth.
The LORD has sworn by His right hand and by the arm of His strength:

"Surely I will no longer give your grain as

food for your enemies;
And the sons of the foreigner shall not drink your new wine, for
which you have labored.
But those who have gathered it shall eat it,
And praise the LORD;
Those who have brought it together shall drink it in My holy courts."
Go through,
Go through the gates!
Prepare the way for the people;
Build up,
Build up the highway!
Take out the stones,
Lift up a banner for the peoples!
Indeed the LORD has proclaimed to the
end of the world:

"Say to the daughter of Zion,
'Surely your salvation is coming; Behold, His reward is with Him,
and His work before Him.'"
And they shall call them The Holy People,
The Redeemed of the LORD;
And you shall be called Sought Out, A
City Not Forsaken.

Let us be people that are rightly adorned—water turned to wine while in our natural vessel, ashes turned to beauty, mourning turned to joy that the oil of gladness be rightly anointing the preparation of the bride.

Let anything that is not rightly dressed for the preparation and celebration of the marriage of the Lamb be removed for the groom of the bride's coming.

Selah

Epilogue

*T*he following Scriptures are an encouragement for you to step out of your comfort zone of traditional teachings on Christianity. As I began my research, the word ALL began to stand out. The Holy Spirit challenged me with the question, "How big is your faith to believe that all really means ALL? The extent of your faith is what will determine ALL in your life. It was then that the Lord reminded me that, *"I could do ALL things through Christ which strengthened me"* (Philippians 4:13).

These Scriptures have been taken from the King James Version of the Bible. The parenthesis are mine, along with capitalizing the word ALL to help you reconsider the way you may have been interpreting our Father's love letters in the past. I encourage you to Peshat, Remez, and Midrash as you enter into Sod, the bridal chamber of Jesus Christ, the throne room of God.

"Which was the son of Enos, which was the son of Seth, which was the son
of Adam, which was the Son of God." (Luke 3:38)

"In the day that God created man, in the likeness (image) *of God* (himself) *made he him: Male and female* (both Adam) *created he them; and blessed them, and called their name Adam, in the day when they were created."* (Genesis 5:1-2)

"And in thee shall ALL families of the earth be blessed." (Genesis 12:3)

"The Lord is gracious, and full of compassion; slow to anger, and of great mercy. The Lord is good to ALL: and his tender mercies are over ALL his works. ALL thy works shall praise thee, O Lord; and thy saints shall bless thee." (Psalm 145:8-10)

"For since by man came death, by man came also the resurrection of the dead. For as in Adam ALL die, even so in Christ shall ALL be made alive." (I Corinthians 15:21-22)

"For it is God which worketh in you both to will and to do of his good pleasure." (Philippians 2:13)

"Do ALL things without murmurings and disputing: That ye may be blameless and harmless, the sons of God, without rebuke, in the midst of a crooked and perverse nation, among whom ye shine as lights in the world." (Philippians 2:14-15)

"Let this mind be in you, which was also in Christ Jesus: Who, being in the form of God, thought it not robbery to be equal with God." (Philippians 2:5-6)

"For the Father judgeth no man, but hath committed all judgment unto the Son." (John 5:22)

"Verily, verily, I say unto you, the Son can do nothing of himself, but what he seeth the Father do: for what things so ever he doeth, these also doeth the Son likewise." (John 5:19)

"ALL things were made by him; and without him was not anything made that was made. In him was life: and the life was the light of men." (John 1:3-4)

"But as many as received him to them gave he power to become the sons of God, even to them that believe on him name." (John 1:12)

"The Lord is not slack concerning his promise, as some men count slackness; but is longsuffering to us-ward, not willing that any should perish, but that ALL should come to repentance." (2 Peter 3:9)

"Not by the works of righteousness which we have done, but according to his mercy he saved us, by the washing of regeneration, and renewing of the Holy Ghost; which he shed on us abundantly through Jesus Christ our Savior; that being justified by his grace, we should be made heirs according to the hope of eternal life." (Titus 3: 5-7)

"Therefore as by the offense of one judgment came upon ALL men to condemnation; even so by the righteousness of one the free gift came upon ALL men unto justification of life." (Romans 5:18)

"There is therefore now no condemnation to them which are in Christ Jesus who walk not after the flesh, but after the Spirit." (Romans 8:1)

"For I am persuaded, that neither death, nor life, nor angels, nor principalities, nor powers, nor things present, nor things to come, nor height, nor depth, nor any other creature, shall be able to separate us from the love of God, which is in Christ Jesus our Lord." (Romans 8:38-39)

"Know ye not that ye are the temple of God, and that the Spirit of God dwelleth in you?" (I Corinthians 3:16)

"Let no man glory in men, For ALL things are yours; whether Paul, or Apollos, or Cephas, or the world, or life, or death, or things present, or things to come; ALL are yours; and ye are Christ's, and Christ is God's." (I Corinthians 3:21-23)

"For by him were ALL things created, that are in heaven, and that are in earth, visible and invisible, whether they be thrones,

or dominions, or principalities, or powers: ALL things were created by him, and for him: and he is before ALL things, and by him ALL things consist." (Colossians 1:16-17)

"And hath made of one blood ALL nations of men for to dwell on all the face of the earth, and hath determined the times before appointed, and the abounds of their habitation; that they should seek the Lord, if haply they might feel after him, and find Him, though he be not far from every one of us: for in him we live, and move, and have our being; as certain also of your own poets have said, for we are also his offspring." (Acts 17:26-28)

"Therefore if any man be in Christ, he is a new creature: old things are passed away; behold ALL things are become new. And ALL things are of God, who hath reconciled us to himself by Jesus Christ, and hath given to us the ministry of reconciliation." (2 Corinthians 5:17-18)

"I am crucified with Christ: nevertheless I live; yet not I, but Christ liveth in me: and the life which I now live in the flesh I live by the faith of the Son of God, who loved me, and gave himself for me." (Galatians 2:20)

"And if ye be Christ's, then are ye Abraham's seed, and heirs according to the promise." (Galatians 3:29)

"And because ye are sons, God hath sent forth the Spirit of his Son into your hearts, crying Abba, Father." (Galatians 4:6)

"Verily, verily, I say unto you, if a man keeps my saying, he shall never see death." (John 8:51)

"Jesus answered them, 'Is not written in your law, I said ye are gods?'" (John 10:34)

"Now is the judgment of this world: now shall the prince of this world be cast out. And I if I be lifted up from the earth will draw ALL men unto me. This he said, signifying what death he should die." (John 12:31-33)

"Therefore, leaving the principles of the doctrine of Christ, let us go on unto perfection; laying again the foundation of repentance from dead works, and of faith toward God, of the doctrine of baptisms, and of laying on of hands, and of resurrection of the dead, and of eternal judgment." (Hebrews 6:1-2)

"We know that we have passed from death unto life, because we love the brethren. He that loveth not his brother abideth in death." (1 John 3:14)

"Ye are of God, little children, and have overcome them: because greater is he that is in you, than he that is in the world." (1 John 4:4)

"Beloved, let us love one another: for love is of God; and every one that loveth is born of God, and knoweth God." (1 John 4:7)

"That which was from the beginning, which we have heard, which we have seen with our eyes, which we have looked upon, and our hands have handled, of the Word of life." (1 John 1:1)

"And these things write we unto you, that your joy may be full. This then is the message which we have heard of him, and declare unto you, that God is light, and in him is no darkness at ALL." (1 John 1:4-5)

"Then Jesus said unto them, 'Yet a little while is the light with you. Walk while ye have the light, lest darkness come upon you: for he that walketh in darkness knoweth not whither he goeth. While ye have light, believe in the light, that ye may be the children of light.'" (John 12:35-36)

"Ye have not chosen me, but I have chosen you, and ordained you, that ye should go and bring forth fruit, and that your fruit should remain: that whatsoever ye shall ask of the Father in my name, he may give it you." (John 15:16)

"Ye are the light of the world. A city that is set on a hill cannot be hid. Let your light so shine before men, that they may see your good works, and glorify your Father which is in heaven." (Matthew 5:14, 16)

"Blessed are the pure in heart: for they shall see God. Blessed are the peacemakers: for they shall be called the children of God." (Matthew 5:8-9)

"Be careful for nothing, but in everything by prayer and supplication with thanksgiving let your requests by made known unto God. And the peace of God, which passeth all understanding, shall keep your hearts and minds through Christ Jesus. Finally, brethren, whatsoever things are true, whatsoever things are honest, whatsoever things are just, whatsoever things are pure, whatsoever things are lovely, whatsoever thing are of good report; if there be any virtue, and if there be any praise, think on these things." (Philippians 3:6-8)

"Rejoice in the Lord always; and again I say, Rejoice." (Philippians 3:4)

"As he is, so are we in this world." (1 John 4:17)

Selah

Appendix

My identity today is in Christ Jesus as a royal priest,
a Holy nation in this world to rule and reign today in Christ according to
His name and nature when I said "I Do."

TODAY, I AM the righteousness of God in Christ Jesus! 2 Corinthians 5:21

TODAY, I AM Blessed with ALL Spiritual blessings in heavenly places! Ephesians 1:3

TODAY, I AM born again by the word of God! 1 Peter 23:1

TODAY, I AM redeemed by the blood! Ephesians 1:7

TODAY, I AM complete in Jesus! Colossians 2:9-10

TODAY, I AM not a sinner. ALL sin identity has been nailed to the cross! Colossians 2:14

TODAY, I AM sealed with the HOLY SPIRIT! Ephesians 1:13

TODAY, I AM ruling and reigning in the name of Jesus! Romans 5:17

TODAY, I AM more than a conqueror! I take dominion! Romans 8:37, Genesis 1:28

TODAY, I AM able to do ALL things through CHRIST who strengthens me! Philippians 4:13

TODAY, I AM strengthened in ALL might by His glorious power! Colossians 1: 9-10

TODAY, I AM able to command the powers of darkness in the name of Jesus! Mark 16:17

TODAY, I AM triumphant in Jesus' name! His word never returns void! I come boldly before the throne of grace receiving unconditional mercy and love. 2 Corinthians 2:14, Isaiah 55:11, Hebrews 4:16

When I know the name of God, I become the duplicate of that name, manifesting those attributes and apprehending that character which the name denotes. This signifies the active presence of His glory: And the WORD BECAME FLESH!

"For As HE is, so am I in this world today"
(1 John 4:17)

Selah

About the Author

Bishop Audrey Drummonds is the founder and director of Interior Coverings Ministry and Outreach Missions in Groveland, Florida, since 2002. She has her PhD in religious philosophy and master's of divinity from Tabernacle Bible College and Seminary, with a bachelor's from Liberty University. She is the presiding bishop of the World Communion of Christian Celtic Convergence Churches into the USA. Ministry has taken her into over forty countries, including Israel, Greece, Turkey, Peru, India, Kenya, Philippines, India, Canada, England, Mexico, Honduras, and Russia. She writes, lectures, teaches, and does public speaking for the ministry's website. She partners and resides with her husband of several real estate developing and construction corporations.

Printed in the United States
by Baker & Taylor Publisher Services